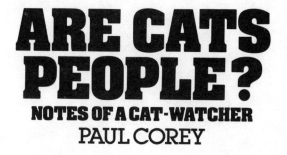

ARE CATS PEOPLE?

NOTES OF A CAT-WATCHER

PAUL COREY

Library of Congress Cataloging in Publication Data

Corey, Paul, 1903-
  Are cats people?

  Includes index.
  1. Cats—Behavior.   I. Title.
SF446.5C66   1979   156   79-50969
ISBN 0-8092-7335-7

Published by Contemporary Books, Inc.
180 North Michigan Avenue, Chicago, Illinois 60601
Manufactured in the United States of America
Library of Congress Catalog Card Number: 79-50969
International Standard Book Number: 0-8092-7335-7

Published simultaneously in Canada by
Beaverbooks
953 Dillingham Road
Pickering, Ontario L1W 1Z7
Canada

Contents

Preface *v*

Acknowledgments *xiii*

Felis Catus Personae *xiv*

1. Is There a Feline IQ? *1*
2. Felis Domestica and the Learning Process *13*
3. Cats and the Conditioned Response Method
   of Learning *25*
4. When Your Cat Talks Do You Listen? *35*
5. Some Notes on Feline Personality *45*
6. Sometimes You Have to Transport Cats *57*
7. What Is Your Cat to You: Pet or Friend? *67*
8. Are Felines Psychic? Or Are Humans Psychotic? *79*
9. We Gave an Abandoned Cat a Home *95*
10. Romance and the Neutered Cat *107*
11. Fun and Games in Feline Society *119*
12. Wildlife and the Feral Cat *135*
13. And Some Go Gently into That Long Sleep *147*
14. The Cat Who Wanted Happenings *161*

Preface

Over the past fifty years I have observed the behavior of sixteen cats, and four of them are still with me. When my book *Do Cats Think?* came out, the question posed in the title elicited a variety of answers. "Of course cats think!" Or, "How stupid? Cats don't think! Only humans think!" And one reviewer wrote, "I *know* cats think! It's people I have my doubts about."

With a title like *Are Cats People?* I can anticipate a similar spread of reactions: "Of course cats are people!" Or, "What sort of weirdo would ask such a question? Only humans are people!" And the cynical reviewer who had no doubts about cats thinking might well say, "The real question is: are *people* people?"

In that comprehensive book, *Cat Catalog*, edited by Judy Fireman, there's an article by Anne Mendelson which states categorically in its title, "Cats Are Not People." Now, I wouldn't hazard a contradiction of such a flat out statement.

She could be right. Then again, it might just be a matter of semantics.

The *Second College Edition of Webster's New World Dictionary* gives as one of ten definitions of "people," a "group of creatures: the ant people." Okay then: why *not* cat people?

I've heard cat lovers say, "My cat thinks he's a people," meaning a person or a human. Or, "My cat thinks he's a dog," meaning that this particular feline likes to go for a walk or stretch out at his owner's feet.

However, if you said of a person, "He thinks he's a dog or a cat or a horse," I would be justified in concluding that he was as freaky as if you said of him, "He think he's Napoleon." There may be cats who think they are other than they really are. If so, I'd consider them as freaky as the person who thinks he's Napoleon.

I've got a fixed belief that a cat not only thinks he's a cat but knows he's a cat. Perhaps some kind of imprinting in kittenhood can make him react to a certain stimulus in such a way that he thinks a dog is a cat, or a chicken is a cat. He may even think that you or I are cats—great god-cats perhaps—but a normal cat simply knows that he *is* a cat. Just the same, it seems to me quite all right if you want to think that your cat thinks he's a people.

This is not a quibble. I'm just trying to put relationships in perspective—the relationship with a cat, dog, horse, neighbor, husband, wife, child. I've chosen the cat because it's easier to miniaturize it as a specific life form for study than all life forms, or all the world, or all the universe. You can choose whatever life form you wish. I'm hooked on cats.

I know that I'm a person. My cats know that they are cats. The basic question is the interrelationship between my cat or cats and me—between cats and humans. That's a minimum view.

The maximum view would be the relationship between all living things. My examination of my relationship with my cats may give me a better view of life—perhaps of living. All relationships are relative—a matter of degree on the part of the interrelating entities, which brings us down to the degree of consciousness of the interrelating entities.

David Hubel and Torsten Wiesel, a couple of Harvard biologists, tried "Observing the brain through a cat's eye." They determined from their experimentation that a cat's "visual-sensitive" period falls within the first three weeks to five months of its life. Any kitten that was not allowed to develop its sight normally during that time became permanently handicapped.

They reached the conclusion that there was "not much difference between us and our feline cousins." The "visual-sensitive" period for human children, they felt, came between the second and fourth year. This was the time of the highest plasticity of the developing brain.

Just as the kitten developed its basic visual capabilities during the first three-weeks-to-five-months span of its life, the human child developed its basic capabilities between the second and fourth years of its life. They concluded that talking to a child in a "wide spectrum of language" during that formative time would enhance its linguistic ability.

Their conclusion on a kitten's sight development seems fairly obvious, and I accept the possibility of a child's linguistic enhancement. But what really excited me was the idea that if a kitten were talked to in a "wide spectrum of language" during the specially sensitive period of its life might it not also develop a special consciousness to human language? Of course it wouldn't know or understand any abstractions in that "wide spectrum" but neither would a four-year-old youngster.

And I wouldn't expect any kitten I tried conversing with to answer me in my language. Feline vocal equipment isn't made for that. But I might enhance the cat's understanding and appreciation of our relationship. It might be possible to raise a kitten's level of word consciousness.

Can't you just hear the "cat haters," and the "scientific minds" snorting: "The guy's gone bananas! He's a hard-core anthropomorphist. Doesn't he know that Man is at the pinnacle of the evolutionary scale?"

Who says so? Opinions vary. A letter from a friend

recently back from a trip to India told about discussing reincarnation with a Hindu. She had said to him, "I know you don't believe that people are punished in future lives by being returned to a lower form. So you wouldn't believe that a person might come back in the form—lower form—of an animal, a cat, say?"

"He sat and thought," she wrote, "then he replied, 'Whoever said that animals are lower than people?'"

But my detractors will argue, "Basic proof that animals are lower is that they have no consciousness."

Consciousness? A moot point. We are told that at the age of six, Julian Jaynes, now a research psychologist at Princeton, stared at a forsythia bush and thought, "How do I know that other people see the same yellow I see?" That was the beginning of his attempt to comprehend consciousness. With the forsythia bush, he had the word "yellow." He could use that word to you or me or anyone else who speaks the same language and we could look at the bush and say, "Yes, I see the same yellow bush you see."

But that's as near as we can come to knowing whether all of us see the *same* yellow. Actually no one ever knows exactly what anyone else sees when he sees the yellow of a forsythia bush. It is the common word we have, "yellow." It is the spoken language that started the development of human consciousness.

Psychologist Jaynes sets forth this concept in his book *The Origin of Consciousness in the Breakdown of the Bicameral Mind.* Before the development of consciousness, even when humans could communicate with one another to a considerable degree, that part of the brain which later housed our emerging consciousness, could pick up commands and hear voices and directives from gods and oracles. Moses received orders from a burning bush; Saint Paul had a directive from a bright light on the road to Damascus; Joan of Arc heard a voice telling her to save France.

Now, perhaps your cat or mine doesn't have a consciousness. But let's assume that it's in a stage of evolving one.

When you see it staring into space or behaving in a strange way, perhaps its bicameral mind is hearing inner voices or commands, or being sense-alerted to the imminence of a storm or earthquake.

Maybe our neutered Siamese, Sci-Fi, got a directive from some cat oracle, telling him to make a pilgrimage through brush and wilderness and canyon to a Priests' Retreat, and then return to his home. He did that and we have no explanation for the trip.

We don't really know whether non-human animals and specifically my cats, or all cats have a consciousness or not. They can communicate with each other in their own language form. Perhaps this is a sign of an emerging consciousness—a cat consciousness. My cats and I have certain language communications between us. Sometimes I understand what they say. More often they understand what I say. Perhaps they have more consciousness than I am aware of.

It was at the age of six that psychologist Jaynes confronted the blooming forsythia and became conscious of its "yellowness." I have felt for a long time that my cats, who are admittedly *advantaged* cats, develop the mental age of a child of five or six. Perhaps if I were more competent to understand their language I would discover that they had a significant consciousness—a consciousness even greater than humans are willing or capable of giving them credit for.

After all, the basic human criterion for intelligence in nonhumans is the ability of the subjects to do tricks and to communicate with humans in the form of the language we humans create. Humans can do tricks but they are too stupid to learn the language of another species.

I can't ask my cats if they see the same yellow I see in the sticky-monkey flower because I don't know how a cat communicates the idea of the color yellow. The scientific know-it-alls will state dogmatically: "Of course cats don't see the same color yellow," without knowing what sticky-monkey flower yellow is. They are ready to assume that yellow is yellow. Actually yellow is a vibration that the retina in the eye picks up and transmits to the brain which interprets it. In what way for a cat, I don't know.

Let's switch to sound, also vibration. A friend of mine had a Siamese named Mae Ling who liked to curl up on his lap while he read. Once when he was preparing for a European trip he had the description of a point of interest in English, French, and German. He read each aloud. Mae Ling slept through the English. When he read the French, she got up with an excited look on her face and slapped his cheek with a soft paw. The German made her get off his lap and stalk out of the room. Her reactions were the same in whatever sequence he read the statements.

What had she heard? Sounds. That's all language is—sounds. We communicate with sound vibrations. They take different shapes and tones. Among humans they have certain meanings—meanings which we give them. What did the sounds Mae Ling heard mean to her?

A recognition of sounds requires a sort of consciousness—or does it? Perhaps the reaction is reflexive. Perhaps the human reaction to sound is reflexive and no evidence of consciousness.

Then there's the fellow who wrote to me about his cat who came from another part of the house or awoke from a sound sleep whenever he used the remote control device to turn on the TV. He himself could hear nothing when he used it, not even a faint click. And his other two cats paid no attention to it. Only this one came, her eyes bright and eager, and she nuzzled the device and purred. Was she getting some message from some cat oracle? Or maybe hers is a consciousness beyond our ken.

I'm not trying to lay any heavy trip on you in this book. It's just that I take my cats and all cats seriously. You can do it with your cats, or your dog, or maybe your wife and kids. Whichever—try observing them and ruminate over what they do and have done. You may learn a lot—maybe about yourself. Speculate about their behavior and postulate hypotheses for their actions.

Dr. Robert Allen Good, when he became president and director of the Sloan-Kettering Institute, said: "Hypotheses are instruments . . . Whether right or wrong doesn't matter. Just trying to find out . . . should force us to think, to examine. That's what science is—or should be—all about."

If that's what science is really all about, we can all play in the same ballpark. Thinking can be an excruciating experience at times, but give it a try. Begin by chucking the Judeo-Christian Ethic that sets Man apart from other animals. Accept yourself as a creature which Shakespeare most accurately called "the paragon of animals."

To consider other living beings, in this case my cats and other cats, as more or less equal is a fun game for me. It needn't be anthropomorphic or sentimental. A sculptor friend of mine yells at her cats, when they sometimes behave as cats do, "Cut it out, will ya! You're acting like people!"

I hope this book, offering my experiences with and observations of "the cat people," and experiences and observations of others, will help cat lovers derive more enjoyment from playing this game with the cats they know.

Acknowledgments

Portions of this book have appeared in
CATS Magazine and *ALL CATS*.

Felis Catus Personae

Leo Primus—"Leo"
Leo Secundus—"Sec"
Leo Tertius—"Tersh"
Leo Quartus—"Leo"
Leo Quintus—"Quin"
Leo Sextus—"Timmy"
Tiki
Topsy
Charles Addams—"Charlie"
Tang
Sci-Fi—"Si"
Curley
Missy
Mao Tse-tung—"Mao"
Missy Manx—"Mitzy" "Bunny"
Benji

1

Is There a Feline IQ?

The term "IQ" (intelligence quotient) is still used to indicate intelligence. IQ tests do not really measure intelligence, but knowledge, and should be specified as "KQ" or knowledge quotient. This misuse has gone on for a long time and has worked to the disadvantage of minorities and ghetto youngsters. The term "IQ" is still used commonly, but the tests, when used at all, are admitted to be only tools to find out a part of intelligence—the knowledge part.

According to the magazine *Psychology Today* a school psychologist in Akron, Ohio has worked up a "Cat-Q." This cat intelligence test is complete with questions, test instruments, and instructions. It might be fun to play around with such a test, but the results are likely to be no more accurate than the findings of the standard IQ test tried on young humans who don't know our language. And the cats, who quite likely will not feel like playing this game, will get a low score.

The knowledge part of intelligence involves words, the

understanding of word meanings and the ability to demonstrate that the subject knows the correct meaning of a word. Words mean language and language means communication. According to psychologist Jaynes, communication means the beginnings of consciousness, the connecting of a word sound with the correct object or subject within a certain "frame of reference." Biologists Hubel and Wiesel feel this accomplishment can be extended by using a wide spectrum of language during the formative period of infancy.

In an attempt to get at the subject of feline KQ, I've put together the words our cats have known or know. You can do the same for the cat or cats you live with. Much depends upon the number of words you use with your cat regularly and the significance of it. A cat's response to a word depends upon his interest in its meaning at a particular moment. Most cats can't be depended on to respond to a word just to please you. It depends upon the degree of interest aroused by the word sound and the frame of reference it fits at the moment.

As you well know, call one cat by its name in the household and all the other cats in the household will come. It may mean food and they're all hungry. Or none will come because none of them are hungry. You probably have special words that are almost always sure to trigger a response.

One of the first words that we became aware of our cats knowing was "catnip." When we lived in Putnam County, N.Y., we had a catnip bush. We called it the "bar" in the summer when the foliage was green. Our cats and the neighborhood cats helped themselves. Many a brawl took place there, not unlike those at a people's bar.

In the fall we dried some of the leaves so our cats could indulge their addiction all winter long. When we offered our first Leo catnip we used the word. In a very short time he knew the sound "catnip" and if we used it in conversation between ourselves or with company and he was present, he would tease for some. So, unless we expected to produce the stuff, we had to spell the word when using it in conversation.

Visitors seemed to think it was a bit strange for us to do that—like spelling "candy" in the presence of a four-year-old to keep it from nagging for some. It was just exactly the same thing.

Our second Leo, Sec, picked up the word sound and meaning from his father, the first Leo. He passed it on to his younger brother Tersh.

When catnip was mentioned, our cats began teasing for it, making a sound like 'murf." It was an eager, joyous sound. The name they gave the herb fit their feelings about it. We began using "murf" to mean "catnip," and shortly we had to spell that too.

Out here in California catnip grew all year and Leo IV and Timmy, who came out here with us, had their fill any time they wanted it. The flourishing bush became a regular place for brawls with the neighborhood cats, usually at cocktail time. Both cats continued to respond to the words "catnip" and "murf" just as they had in Putnam County.

Tiki, our first Siamese, picked up those words from Timmy, the last of our New York red tabbies. Later, Tiki's sister Topsy learned the words when she came to live with us. However, Tang, our third Siamese and the cat to live longest with us; and Charles Addams, a black-and-white barn cat, found no meaning in the words because neither of them cared for the stuff.

Our latest Siamese, Mao, and our first Burmese, Benji, are both addicts. Ruth has tried to revive the words, but with only moderate success. The herb is too available to have any special meaning to them.

Curley, our present red tabby, doesn't care for catnip, and neither does Missy Manx. She soon learned that when Mao stopped at the "bar" and began getting "high" he'd chase her. So, whenever she saw him heading that way she promptly got lost.

One of the words Tang knew which we had to spell or face pestering to produce one, was "gopher." He caught them and they were high on his gourmet list. I trapped them and gave them to him. I used a "kill" trap, but checked it frequently to make sure it did its job or I could give the *coup de grace* and eliminate unnecessary suffering.

After catching a couple for him, he expected me to produce one every day. At the time I usually brought a gopher in, he'd begin teasing me to produce. "No luck today, Tang. I didn't get one this time, man." It took a lot of talk to quiet him down.

He would keep it up until he got interested in something else. I don't know whether he was "just fussing" and his talk and mine had no meaning to him in a language sense, or my soothing sounds helped calm his aroused hunger.

We have to spell "walk" in the presence of all of our cats unless a real walk is intended. In the summer it was usually too hot for our cats to walk except in the evenings when Ruth and I both went on such strolls. In winter, here in California, with favorable weather, Ruth took them on a walk around our few acres or up the ridge into the woods almost daily. It was her way to get some exercise and fresh air, and see what was going on in the world of *shooting stars* and *wild iris*.

Cats like to go for walks with people. They don't use the occasion, like dogs, as an excuse to range and hunt and perhaps kill. Our cats stay close to us. If we stop to examine a flower, they join us and smell it. If we stop to rest, have a cigarette, or just view the scenery, they find comfortable spots and wait until we move on.

I think cats like to walk with people because it makes them feel that at last these humans are behaving a little more like cats.

A word our cats learned quickly is "no!" Although they don't always respond. Sometimes they're testing us; sometimes they may not see any sense to our use of it as it applies to them. "Out" is another word they pick up at an early age. Other words we use sometimes take on different interpretations to our cats.

After Timmy and Tiki ambushed a stray cat that came into our kitchen and stole a leg of lamb, Ruth began calling such strays "badcat." Later, Charles and Tang were reluctant to confront any strange cat that came around. Topsy, the oldest and number one cat at this time, always reacted. At the mention of "badcat" she immediately made a check of the kitchen and the immediate outdoors to locate this possible miscreant. If any strange cat tried to enter her domain, she beat the hell out of it.

When any of our cats misbehaved they were also called a "bad cat" and the word with its dual meaning has come down to the present. Once Ruth tried to castigate Mao for some mischief by calling him a "bad cat." He began looking all around and out windows searching for this "bad cat" she was talking about. He could not see himself as the culprit and I don't know if he appreciated the humor in his actions or not.

Cats react best to simple short names. Our black-and-white Charlie once made it quite clear he knew his name in spite of his barncat background. Late one evening, Ruth and I were discussing poetry, poets and editors. We mentioned John Ciardi, a fine poet and poetry editor of *The Saturday Review* in its heyday. We mentioned his name a number of times. Charlie was asleep on a red boucle-covered chair. When I went to the bookshelves for one of Ciardi's books, Charlie roused up and began talking, miaowing loudly and clearly and insistently, his wide eyes following me as I crossed the room.

On my return, I stopped and said to him, "Charlie, what's the matter with you? What are you talking about?"

He repeated the sounds he had been making emphatically.

Ruth said, "It's the name Ciardi. He thinks we've been saying 'Charlie,' and he keeps telling us that he's right here. He thinks we're nuts."

We then called the poet by his first name, "John," and Charlie went back to sleep.

Our present red tabby, Curley, was the subject of a different name incident. We knew practically nothing about his life before he strayed into our patio. He seemed to accept the name Curley and he comes when we use it. All cats, no matter what their names, will come if they think food is involved. And Curley, who had to scrounge a living before he found us, was always interested in any sound that might have something to eat at the end of it.

One day when Ruth called him he didn't respond so she called, "Kitty-kitty. Kitty-kitty." He pricked up his ears and came running. He had never shown such an eager response before.

She speculated that as a young cat and during his life of scrounging, anyone who seemed at all friendly had called him "Kitty-kitty." That may have been all he was ever called during his early "formative" kitten months. We still call him Curley, but when we want prompt action we call, "Kitty-kitty."

After Charlie was killed, if we mentioned his name in Tang's presence, he'd start talking to us. We tried to explain that Charlie was dead and wasn't coming back. It did no good and he'd go out of doors and roam about the ranch calling.

When Charlie was alive we felt Tang hassled him. His reaction to Charlie's name became more than we could take. So we changed to saying the "black-and-white," or "C" or simply "his friend," indicating the Siamese with a nod.

I don't know how cats communicate the fact of "death" to each other. We never recovered Charlie's body so all Tang knew, as far as we could tell, was that Charlie was gone. He'd been gone before and returned. If I knew what a cat meant by "dead," and could have told him, perhaps he would have understood. Then again, perhaps he knew that his black-and-white companion was dead and he was simply mourning him. My uncertainty of whether or not my cats understand the word "dead" seems to me to be a serious interspecies failure in communication. All-knowing psychologists will say, "That's the difference between animals and humans," meaning in the context of the Judeo-Christian Ethic, human animals and non-human animals. Humans can understand abstractions. They can understand the abstraction *death*." But how can we assume that a cat doesn't understand abstractions? We don't know a cat's language.

It is difficult to look into another person's mind and understand what goes on there even with one's own mind as a guide, and a language to facilitate communication. My assumption is that the mammalian brains differ only in degrees. So without word communication it is almost impossible to understand what goes on in another mind—in a cat's mind, in a cat's consciousness.Short of the overlay of religion, after-life, reincarnation and such unprovable hypotheses, the only thing a brain knows about *death* is that the animate has become inanimate—the warm has become cold. We can go into the subject of the cessation of heartbeats and brain waves, but these are details.

Our red tabby, Leo III, or Tersh, didn't know such details about death, but he knew simple facts. When the young rabbit he had caught no longer screeched, it was a condition that the human (me) found acceptable, that I didn't scold him about, and he proceeded to eat it. He knew when a mouse was dead. He knew when it was warm-dead and he could eat it, and when it was cold-dead, stale, and inedible. A human may know many more details about the state of being dead than a feline knows, such as having a word for the condition "dead" but the basic understanding of the abstraction is the same. The problem is simply communication.

When Tersh's older brother Sec didn't come back we had no way of conveying the meaning of the words, "Sec is dead," to him. We could say, "Sec isn't coming back." But his brother had been gone before and returned. Perhaps we'd bring him back from the vet in the Ford truck, or he'd just come back from one of his forays as he had many times. A year or several years later, Tersh would have accepted him as if he had only been away a few days. The stimulus that meant a living Sec in Tersh's brain would have programmed the same reaction it had always produced.

It's quite possible that Tersh knew the word "dead." We had used the word to him. He could have learned it through repetition and association with a dead body, which is the pattern learning takes in a brain whether feline or human.

We had no way of tying this abstraction to the absence of his brother in his mind. There was no *corpus delicti*. As far as Tersh was concerned, his brother Sec was not dead, but had just gone away.

The same situation abided with Tang in the absence of Charlie. To him, Charlie was away. Since I could not communicate the real situation, Tang was only aware of missing his black-and-white companion.

Someone is sure to say, "He wouldn't know how long his friend would be away, or had been away, if he returned. That's the difference between humans and animals." A phrase for that is "time-binding."

The basic mistake here is the assumption that *time*, like Athena, sprang forth fully conceived and detailed from Man's mind. Fact is, *time* was created, probably along with psychologist Jaynes' consciousness, when Man needed something to help him organize his life as it became more complicated. The human brain, a computer, a machine, is extremely intricate and beset by increasing numbers and kinds of input. It is so complex that the feedback and retrieval mechanism can break down under programming. The creation of *time* was a way to simplify certain retrieval operations.

A feline brain is basically the same as the human brain, also a computer, but we assume it hasn't nearly as much input which makes recall simpler. Yet a cat will "bind time" when the binding helps him organize his life to his liking. If a cat likes some action, food or a walk at a particular time of day, he will let the human know when that time arrives. And it isn't the position of the sun because he'll make known his wishes on a cloudy day.

Time is also involved in goings and comings. It can mean a lot to a cat, perhaps more than we suspect. Once, when Charlie was still alive, I'm sure that a simple way of conveying the meaning of "death," such as showing a dead body could have saved both Charlie and Tang considerable cat concern and unhappiness.

The disruption of a closely-knit family of cats and humans

such as ours can bring out as much of a show of love and loss in the cats as it can in the people involved.

Several years after we had moved into our second and present home here in California, Topsy, our second Siamese, became seriously ill. We weren't completely aware of the problem. She was five years older than Tang and Charlie. She and Tang often played together like kittens, even that last year. She would initiate the game. She had never been ill at any time in her life, except for a bad tooth. However, from time to time, for no apparent reason she would make loud, harsh Siamese cries. It was as if she felt a severe pain. If we consoled her and talked and petted her, she responded by rubbing against us, butting and purring. As summer approached this year she seemed worse and I took her to our vet. He couldn't determine anything in particular wrong with her. He gave her an antibiotic injection and me some pills to give her.

Topsy was one of the worst cats I've ever known to give pills to, but I did manage to get one pill down her. She didn't spit it out. She vomited. Along with the pill came some stuff that looked like ribbon macaroni. I took her to the vet again. He said she had tapeworm and tried to deworm her but she showed no improvement. In fact her cries became worse and since it was a weekend I couldn't contact the vet. If I had known some way to put her out of her misery short of bludgeoning her with the fireplace poker, I would have done it.

That Sunday night Ruth stayed up with her on the couch in the family room, talking to her, petting and soothing her when she cried out. This seemed to assuage the pain a little or distract her from it. Monday, as soon as the vet's office was open, we took her in. The doctor suspected intenstinal blockage, perhaps cancer. Topsy crouched on the examining table motionless.

"She doesn't care anymore," he said.

The agony was all too plain in her eyes. And it isn't anthropomorphic to say so. I asked the vet to put her to sleep.

Then I did what I now consider to be a thoughtless act. Tang and Charles weren't around when we got home. I didn't call them to see and sniff Topsy's dead body. We were so wrapped up in our own misery, assuming probably that cats couldn't understand and feel such an abstract thing as sorrow over her death. I buried her without considering them.

Did it really matter at all? They were just two cats.

But Tang and Charlie had known from her cries that she was in trouble. They knew when I put her in the carrier and took her to the vet and brought her back the first time. I took her to the vet a second time but as far as they knew, or as far as we were aware of their knowing, she had not come back that last time.

Had we given her away? That was an experience within Tang's frame of reference. Always before we had brought Topsy back but this time we hadn't. We didn't talk to them about it. We were too miserable. We didn't say to them, "Topsy's dead." Death is an abstraction—remember? We didn't let them see the stiff little body—the only means of communicating this abstraction to them.

Can anything like that really matter to a cat? I didn't give the idea much thought at the time.

Six weeks later Ruth went into the hospital for surgery. I took her in the car. Both cats knew she had gone with me. We often went in the car together. I returned without her. We had always left together and come back together, except once when Ruth visited our daughter for six weeks. But at that time, Tang and Charlie didn't have the experience of one of their family, Topsy, going away in the car and not coming back. This was a new thing to them. Now Ruth had gone away and I didn't bring her back.

During the days that followed when alone at home Tang was always near me and, unusually often, so was Charlie. They were there to greet me when I returned from shopping or visiting Ruth in the hospital. When I read in the evenings or watched TV, Tang slept on my lap, which wasn't unusual, but Charlie lay at my feet, paws folded beneath him, and that *was* unusual. They didn't seem to want to let me out of their sight.

Between our bedroom and bath is a sliding screen which opens from the bath into the patio. During the night, if I went to the bathroom, one of the cats would let me know he was out in the patio. From there he could see me in bed. In the morning, there was always one or the other sitting out there.

When I told Ruth about it, she said, "They think you left me at the vet just as they think we did Topsy. They don't know any different. They feel that they've lost Topsy, and they've lost me, and now they're afraid they might lose you too." Such speculation was good for a laugh. Such funny little characters cats are. They couldn't possibly show such a depth of feeling.

Ruth was in the hospital for nine days. I brought her home just before lunch. Tang was out behind the house. The moment he heard her voice, he came charging in, talking frantically at the top of his Siamese lungs. He rubbed against her, butted her, refused to let her out of his sight. She couldn't even go to the bathroom without him following. Many cats are bathroom goers with people, but Tang wasn't one of them except on this occasion.

Charlie came in, unusual for him at lunch time, rubbed against Ruth and butted her. He wasn't nearly as demonstrative as Tang, but still very demonstrative for him. He didn't have Tang's frame of reference of being "given away" after he was a grown cat. Now Ruth whom he thought had been given away or left at the vet's, was back again.

After lunch, when Ruth lay down in the guest room for a nap, Tang insisted on sleeping with her. He insisted on going to bed with her that night. He had never done that before and we didn't permit our cats to sleep with us as a regular thing.

The next day, apparently satisfied that Ruth was home to stay—perhaps feeling that the plague of family disappearances had been broken—he resumed his normal routine of eating and sleeping. He didn't pay any more attention to her than usual. Whether in his mind and Charlie's the conclusion had been reached that since Ruth had come back, maybe Topsy would return some day, there was no way of knowing.

Perhaps the depth of feline IQ or KQ is limited by the human inability to understand and communicate with them. This condition is circumscribed by the human attitude that non-human animals are abysmally low on the learning scale. It is easy for Man to underestimate a cat's ability to learn because Man uses the same measurements for feline learning that he uses for human learning.

2

Felis Domestica and the Learning Process

Most humans, being self-oriented, feel that any mammal who doesn't try to act like a human is *ipso facto* stupid. In this intelligence comparison game cats get very low marks. Of all domestic mammals, felines show the greatest resistance to behaving like humans.

Dr. Frank Miller's daily syndicated veterinary column printed a letter which stated, "A girl I know who has a lot of cats was trying to tell me cats are as smart as monkeys. Can you give me any proven examples of this? I doubt it."

Dr. Miller replied, "It would be foolish to attempt to make a monkey out of a cat. However, one of the areas in which cats demonstrate learning attributed formerly only to primates is that of learning by observation, a process not easy for animals. Yet aside from the primates, felines are the first and only species proven in the laboratory to perform tasks faster when they've been allowed to watch others in the learning process."

In observing our cats, I discovered years ago to my surprise, that kittens coming into the family learned the protocol of the house from the cats in residence. Only the cats we acquired who were past that formative five-month period of kittenhood (determined by biologists Hubel and Wiesel) showed resistance to established behavior in the family. Then, the resident cats sometimes picked up bad habits from the newcomer.

Two cats, Tang, a Siamese, and Benji, a Burmese, were at least two years old when their owners gave them to us. Indoctrination into the dos and don'ts of the house took a long time and neither ever thoroughly accepted them. We had one exception. Curley, our present red tabby, was an abandoned cat and wanted a home desperately. He breeched protocol occasionally after we took him in but he picked up the local feline customs quickly and seldom broke them later.

When a cat wants to do something he sees another cat do, the learning process is almost instantaneous. It is as if the actions of one programs the correct response in the brain of the other.

Forty years ago in our second house in Putnam County, New York, our bedroom window with the cat ladder up to it presented us with insect problems. The steel casement sash swung out. If I used the screen provided, the cats were shut out. In the winter I could remove the screen and the cold weather took care of the bugs. In spring, summer and fall the New England climate provided a full quota of winged, stinging and biting insects. As a solution I built a wood-framed screen to fit this bedroom window. On the side of one out-swinging sash I put a 5"x8" screen panel at the bottom of the overall frame, and hinged at the top edge so that when the glass sash swung out, the small screen panel would swing freely in and out.

I wasn't certain how to introduce this new way of ingress and egress to the cats. At the time they were Leo IV and Leo Quintus, Quin for short. Quin was the only cat around so I took him upstairs, let him sniff the swinging screen, flipped it in and out for him several times, then pushed him gently through the opening. He stood on the landing at the top of the ladder, looked around, flirted his tail; then I called him back into the house, helping him a little by lifting the panel by the corner. I pushed him through again and repeated this routine. After that I took him downstairs and put him out the front door. If he wanted to come back in, he'd have to go around the house, climb the ladder as usual, and negotiate the swinging screen on his own.

I waited to see what would happen. At dinner time we heard a commotion on the cat ladder. It could have been Quin and Leo playing. Sometimes they tried to keep each other off the ladder. Or, one or the other might try to bring a catch up the ladder and into the house.

Before either Ruth or I could get to the kitchen window for a look, we heard galloping feet across our bedroom above the kitchen and down the stairway. Here came Quin, and damn-the-torpedoes. He stopped on the landing at the foot of the stairs, a look of sheer exuberance on his red tabby face. Then he spun around and raced back up the stairs. We heard him gallop through our bedroom again. A pause followed; apparently he was negotiating the screen panel, and out and down the ladder he plummeted. Before he reached the ground, he stopped, turned back, thumped up the ladder, dived through the swinging screen this time without hesitation, and galloped across the bedroom and down the stairs again. This was a game to him. He repeated the performance several more times before he tired of it.

At that time I wasn't aware of the impressionistic early five months in a cat's life, but Quin had a few weeks of that period to go. I didn't have to show Leo how to use the trick screen. He must have picked it up by watching Quin.

As long as you let your cats set up their own routines and follow them they'll be happy. But if you try to break this pattern you may find yourself in trouble. Perhaps one or another of your cats has observed the way you do something and can top you.

Out here in California, our cats had their own entrance and exit arrangement. At first it was relatively simple. A two-way swinging screen panel let them in from the deck to a screened-in porch; from there into the dining-room-kitchen was more complicated. The dining table stood close to a pair of sliding glass doors. When complete freedom of coming and going was allowed, the double doors were shoved aside to expose a gap of six inches between one door sash and the door jamb at that side. I fastened a 1"x 6" board on edge to the door sash. It was eight inches from reaching the floor so a 6"x 8" opening let the cats come into the house.

That was all right much of the time but a hole that size could let in a lot of cold air in the winter.

I ordered a Flexport Pet Door, an oval arrangement of transparent plastic leaves, the center of which the pet pushes through to enter and the leaves close behind him. I installed it in the 6"x8" opening in the side of the door confident that the cats would use it and the cold air would be kept out.

In winter, and when cold outside, we closed the double doors. When a cat wanted in, it came through the swinging screen panel into the porch and sat in front of the doors until someone in the family saw it and pulled the doors apart far enough to let it come in. At meal time I sat at the end of the dining table and could reach one of the horizontal rails of the glass doors to pull it back far enough to let the waiting cat in. Then I pushed it closed again. So, only at night, or when we were away, were the doors shoved aside, and the small opening for the cats used.

At this time our cats were Topsy and Tang, Siamese, and Charles Addams, black-and-white. After I put in this new gadget they refused to use it. Their attitude, like that of all cats, was conservative toward any innovation. They were accustomed to a setup with a swinging screen which they could see through before venturing forth, and an inside opening that had no visual obstruction until I put in this flexport. The plastic is transparent, but apparently not clear enough. I made a concession by removing one of the plastic leaves. This allowed them to see through sufficiently to satisfy their cautiousness. They accepted it. After they had used this modified flexport for a while I planned to put back the missing section, thinking they would accept the whole thing. One Sunday when we were going to visit some friends, I noted that all three of the cats were out. I put in the missing section, pulled the glass doors together and the entire unit to one side, exposing the flexport. This was the usual way we left the cats' entrance, only this time all the plastic leaves were in place. When they got hungry enough, I assured myself, and with their food in the kitchen, they would have to accept the new arrangement and come in. We arrived home at eleven o'clock and all three cats were in the kitchen. They greeted us and I felt a moment of triumph. Then I noticed the double glass doors. They were separated at the center, just wide enough to let a cat through, all three cats through.

I was fairly sure who was responsible for frustrating me, that seal-point character, Tang. He was a tough-minded cat, not about to accept any new routine that could be circumvented. Many times he had watched me sit at the end of the dining table, reach up and slide half of the glass door pair back to let him in or out.

Most non-cat folk fail to realize how acutely a cat observes anything that interests him. Many cat owners will tell you how their cat will stand up and try to turn a doorknob the way he's seen humans do it. Cats can learn to open a door with a lever type latch. Cats have been known to ring doorbells and bang knockers to get someone to let them in.

Our rear screendoor was loose at the bottom. Mao, our present Siamese, learned to hook a corner and bang it until I came to let him in. The door is right next to his own flexport. I finally got tired of giving him doorman service and tightened the screen so he couldn't bang it. He returned to using the flexport without complaining.

There's a variety of routines cats pick up by observing. *The Basic Book Of The Cat* tells of a firehouse cat in Long Beach, California who is always the first one to slide down the pole when the alarm sounds.

Most cats like to follow people into bathrooms. I suppose it's a kind of voyeurism. But many city cats have learned to use bathroom toilets. There are methods of training cats to use people-toilets instead of litterboxes. They can learn this quite on their own—apparently from watching humans.

Our friend, Laurie Huff, had a Siamese named Beanie who used the human toilet. He didn't have a special catdoor so when he was outside hunting, playing or exploring and had to "go" he came to the house door and scratched to be let in. He'd go to the bathroom, use the toilet, then ask Laurie to let him outdoors again. If the bathroom door happened to be closed or someone had thoughtlessly put down the toilet lid, Beanie would let out a blast of Siamese that let the world know his indignation at such inconsiderate human behavior.

Cats pick up directions just by observing the movement of a finger. My desk is beside a window wall fronting on our deck. More than halfway along this wall is the sliding door opening from the living room. Quite often Tang came up on the deck and sat outside the window and stared at me while I worked.

Sometimes he just wanted me to turn on the sun if it was a foggy morning and sometimes he wanted me to let him in. One day to be sure "in" was what he wanted, I made direct eye-contact with him, then conspicuously pointed toward the sliding door. He immediately got up and went to the door. I left my chair and let him in.

At the time I considered the incident a fluke. Tang had concluded from the movement of my hand, finger pointing, that I was going to get up and let him in, and what my finger indicated had nothing to do with his going over to the door. Then Shirley Keith in Santa Barbara wrote to me about her cats Gulliver and Penny. Both cats were big and Shirley is small. Penny bossed the house and if she got on Shirley's lap first she wouldn't let Gulliver on.

One time when Shirley lay on the couch, Penny had stretched out comfortably, taking all the space from waist to knees. There was still room for Gul on Shirley's chest. Gul was afraid to jump up because Penny would certainly bat him down. Shirley watched him sitting on the floor looking forlorn. Finally she felt sorry for him. She made contact with his eyes, then pointed from him to the end of the couch; from there along the top of the back of the couch to just above her chest, then down to the unoccupied space. She repeated the pantomime.

Gulliver pondered, washed a shoulder, then casually leaped to the arm of the couch. There he hesitated, looked all around but not at Penny. He stretched, then as if going for a stroll walked along the top of the couch back. He stopped above Shirley's chest, looked up at the ceiling and around before coming quietly down and curling up on the vacant space comfortably. Penny probably knew what was going on all the time but Gul carried out the maneuver in such a way that she couldn't find an excuse to object.

One of the basic arguments used by dog lovers to prove that the canine brain is superior to the feline brain is that dogs learn tricks. True. A cat can be taught tricks but he resists the idea. A contemporary Canadian novelist, Robertson Davies, says that dogs are "yes-animals for those too poor to afford yes-men." A cat is not a "yes-animal." But that doesn't mean he doesn't like to perform. On the contrary, cats are great "hams," at least some are.

Probably the best known pair of animal trainers today are Moe Dviesso and his wife Nora. They believe that with "rewards, patience and love there is no animal that cannot be trained." They have trained many of the cats for the cat commercials we see on TV.

Ted and Pat Derby used this "kindness" method in training their animals. They added the idea of letting their animals come up with tricks of their own and helped them make the most of what the animal wanted to do. And they never made one of their animals act if that animal indicated that it didn't feel like it. The Derbys, like the Disessos, never let any of their animals act under hazardous conditions.

This method of animal training is well-known in the USSR. The career of Yuri Kuklachev is a good example of how it worked with cats. He was only a mediocre juggler with the Moscow Circus. Then, when his group was playing in Cherkassy, he picked up a bedraggled stray kitten and took her home. He cleaned her up, fed her and became very fond of her. He called her Strelka (arrow). She got along with the dog he had in his juggling act and seemed to like to watch them when they performed.

One day, Strelka couldn't be found. Yuri searched the house and finally found her curled up asleep in a large clean cooking pot on the stove. He took her out and lectured her on her choice of sleeping quarters. She flirted her tail defiantly, leaped back on the stove and into the pot to resume her nap.

That changed Yuri's act. He became a stage-chef. His act opens with him finding Strelka in the cooking pot. From the beginning Strelka enlarged the act, working out new routines such as attacking the seat of Yuri's trousers during a performance, and doing other tricks which she came up with on her own and played for fun. She trained other cats who learned from watching her and were brought into the act. Now Yuri and his cats are circus stars.

When we moved into our second house in Putnam County, we had a large, round bowl eight inches deep, nine inches across with a five-and-a-half-inch opening. It sat on a wide front window ledge. Quin used it for a game. He'd race around the living room and kitchen, leap to the window ledge and dive into the bowl. Gone, vanished completely. Then up would come his orange-yellow head like a jack-in-the-box, eyes wild and bright. We laughed at him and he loved it.

Whether it's for laughs or some advantage to itself, the cat will learn the necessary tricks fast and it doesn't need a teacher. Ms. Eloise Keeler, in her column on pets, reported that a cat she knew learned to open the cupboard door to get at the dry pet food. There isn't anything very remarkable about that, but after eating her fill, this cat closed the door again so that the family dog couldn't get into the dry food.

In another of her columns, Ms. Keeler reported that "Happi Cat, a tabby owned by fourteen-year-old Candy Hunke of Campbell, California, takes her toys out of their basket for Candy to toss for her to retrieve and after she's tired of playing with them puts them back in the basket."

I don't blame you if you're skeptical of these anecdotes. Yet they might not be exaggerations. I've known cats to open doors. If any door in our house was not latched tightly, Tang would open it and come through trumpeting loudly and triumphantly that we hadn't latched it properly. I don't know if his brain failed to register the click of a firmly latched door or he automatically went around checking doors to make sure they were closed. However, I've never known a cat to close a door after he'd gone through.

I've known cats to get out toys to play with but not put them back. Beanie used a bathroom toilet, and I've known other cats to use bathroom toilets, but I've never known a cat to flush it after using it. Nevertheless, Jo and Paul Loeb in their book *You Can Train Your Cat* insist that a cat can be taught to flush the "john" after using it.

Retrieving is one of the easier tricks that kittens pick up. That is, if they feel like it. It fits well into their natural game interest. Ming, a ten-month-old Siamese, was left with us for several weeks by some friends. To amuse him, Ruth twisted up an empty cigarette package and threw it for him to chase. Very quickly he learned to bring it back to her so that she could throw it again.

Once when she tired of the game, she said, "Take it to Paul," when he brought it back. I was on the couch. He picked it up again, brought it over and laid it on the floor in front of me. When I threw it, he brought it to me after that. This only happened once. His people came for him before we could find out if we could change his game players on command .

Some tricks cats come up with are quite complicated for them to work out and are not repeated. Our daughter Anne and her husband George had two Siamese, Tiki and Tom.

One evening George was typing a paper and the two young cats, six or seven months old, were playing around the couch where he worked. On impulse, George put the rigid cover for the portable typewriter over Tiki as he wiggled his butt ready to pounce from the couch upon Tom. This drew Tom's attention and he tried to get at Tiki beneath the cover. After several attempts from the front side, he got up on the couch between the cover and the back and pushed with his body until one side of the cover stuck out over the front edge of the seat. Then he jumped down to the floor and worked himself up through the narrow space made by the overhanging part of the cover and joined Tiki beneath it.

If a cat comes up with a game that appeals to him he'll repeat it whenever he feels like having some fun. At the time Leo IV was a kitten, we were raising rabbits. Whenever I butchered one, I saved the tail, dried it and gave it to the cats to play with. Leo made a game with one I gave him and I feel sure that he did it solely for our benefit. We were living in our first cottage at the time and worked and read in a long glassed-in porch.

Sometimes as we were reading, Leo would start racing around the house carrying his white rabbit tail. Ruth usually reclined on a daybed, propped up against cushions. I sat on the opposite side of our oil lamp in the first chair I ever built. We both faced the end of the couch-bed.

After Leo's racing and racket had attracted our attention, an abrupt silence followed. We waited. It was like listening for the second shoe to fall. Then up over the end of the couch Leo would appear, just his head, with the rabbit tail in his mouth, tip pointing down, making him look like a Kentucky fried chicken colonel. He'd hold that pose, giving us a wild look, then he'd disappear. More racket in the other part of the house followed by silence. Again he'd appear at the foot of the couch. This time the rabbit tail would be crosswise in his mouth like a moustache.

A few repetitions of that routine and we would be laughing hysterically. That seemed to be all he wanted: his audience rolling in the aisles. When he tired of entertaining us, he'd settle down, hold the rabbit tail between his front paws and wash it carefully. Then he'd fall asleep.

Our cats had rabbit tail toys long after we had stopped raising rabbits because I couldn't face the butchering job. But they were one of many things that made me realize a cat needs only opportunity and necessity to learn tricks that please him, and are within his physical capabilities.

3

Cats and the Conditioned Response Method of Learning

As I understand it, when a living being is born, the genes of ancestors set the pattern of the individual. From then on, the environment, working on this pattern, shapes the growing character. This is conditioning.

A human or non-human can be conditioned to like something or to do something because of pleasant and kindly treatment. They can also be conditioned not to like or do something by some painful experience. That's why the "electric shock" treatment, or the "insulin shock" treatment get into some institutions treating mentally disturbed humans. That's why the whip, the gun and the cattleprod get into the training of non-human animals to do something they were not intended by nature to do.

If the word "instinct" is to have real meaning, it must cover a living being's first innate response to hunger, fear, pain and love. Hunger means the stomach is empty. Fear covers loud noises and the sensation of falling. Pain is the reaction to any damage to the nervous system. Love is the reaction to soothing, pleasant treatment.

Humans have learned to manipulate all of these to get their way with humans and non-humans alike. Sometimes it is preplanned but many times the conditioning is accidental. All living beings have hangups of one kind or another, but not many know what violent or pleasant experience was responsible for such hangups.

We are told that when Bob Martwick took the big red tabby from the cage at the Hinsdale Humane Society shelter, he placed him on the concrete floor. Then he dropped an empty tin food plate. Most cats would have panicked at the loud clang. But this red tabby gave a "so what " reaction, and that started his career as 9 Lives' famous Morris. What conditioned him to accept such a loud noise no one knows and Morris never told. Perhaps he was born in a boiler factory or a steel mill.

The only heat we had in the first unit of the house I was building here in California was a fireplace. Our land had a lot of dead manzanita trees, and the stumps came loose easily. However, some of these stumps had root ends sticking out which were extremely hard.

In our restricted quarters I had placed a cot against the wall between the fireplace and the hallway to the front door. Getting one of those stumps with its bristling root stubs through the front door, down the hallway and around to the fireplace was quite a struggle. Leo liked to sleep on this cot in the daytime. Once when I brought in a stump he was curled up there. He raised his head just as I made the turn from the hallway toward the hearth. I wasn't moving quickly, but a root stub struck him in the center of the forehead. The blow almost knocked him cold. He rolled off the bed and floundered drunkenly into the kitchen.

I unloaded the stump, followed him, apologizing for what I had done, talking soothingly and petting him. He recovered quickly and showed no indication that he blamed me for what had happened.

After that I could come into the house, down the hallway

and make the turn to pass the cot and he wouldn't budge. If I had even a small stick in my hands, he'd take off in terror. No amount of cajoling, explaining or petting could exorcise that conditioned response.

Sometimes our cats have hangups and I've been at a loss to know where the conditioning came from. Several have developed panic reactions from sharp metallic sounds, due perhaps to the sound of the cage door closing when they were in the veterinary hospital to be neutered. I've often thought that such cages should have pads or rubber bumpers so that the closing would be soundless.

Such was the source of Charles Addams' flight reaction when I closed the transom above the windows in the second house I built here in California. Whenever I picked up the pole I used to open or close them he would dash for the flexport in panic. I knew of no excuse for him to be terrified of the pole, but the opening or closing of the transom was accompanied by a sharp metallic click.

A friend of ours who visited us in California almost every year for from two weeks to a month, had a very heavy voice. Charles wasn't afraid of him as long as he spoke softly. If he spoke in his normal voice, Charlie would take off for outdoors. The only explanation we could come up with for such behavior was our vet who neutered him. He had a deep voice and we assumed that Charlie associated our friend's voice with that of this doctor.

Voice sounds can have an opposite effect. Jerre Mangione, a friend of ours, has a rich, vibrant voice. He visited us and began relating some anecdote. Our fourth Leo sat on his haunches in front of the buffet, staring up at him, entranced by the sound of his voice. Such attention unnerved Jerre. He stopped his story and demanded, "What's that cat staring at me for?"

Ruth explained that Leo just loved Jerre's voice. We had to put Leo outdoors before Jerre would finish his story.

The sound of music affects many animals. When we played our phonograph in Putnam County our first red tabbies became amorous. If we played a certain Caruso record on the terrace of our cottage the neighbor's cow would come galloping across the pasture, lean over the fence and moo forlornly. Here in California when Ruth plays the piano our cats collect as close to her as possible to listen and watch.

Somewhere in their kittenhood they were conditioned to like musical sounds. But John D. MacDonald in his great cat book *The House Guest* tells about bringing home a soprano saxophone. When he played it, his two cats, Roj and Geoff, would howl like dogs. Perhaps the higher pitch of the instrument hurt their ears.

We taught our first cats to respond to whistling. It's not uncommon for people to whistle for their children, dogs and horses. Susan deTreville, a friend working on the California Mountain Lion Program, lived in a cabin in the Willow Creek Canyon of Los Padres National Forest. She kept her horse, Paco, in a makeshift corral. He got out. When she went to find him she tried to whistle him up and got a reply. She thought some bird was imitating her call. On the way back to the cabin after catching Paco, she saw mountain lion tracks in the trail dust. She had been followed. It is customary for mountain lions to whistle to their cubs and to each other. Susan had a moment of fright although she was well aware that mountain lions won't attack humans unless they are sick or threatened.

Not all cats are conditioned to the sound of whistling. Once when Ruth was in bed with a cracked pelvis, she needed a way to call me if I happened to be outdoors. We remembered the whistle she had used as a teacher. She tried it out and our Burmese, Benji, went flying out of the room in terror. He seemed highly incensed by her use of it and wouldn't go near her for days. Our other cats were startled by the shrill sound, but he was outraged. It had obviously hurt his ears.

We considered it as a disciplining device when he got on a climbing rampage. The next time he leaped to the top of the refrigerator I blew it. He leaped down in terror. The strange result of the incident was that he didn't hold the act against me but blamed Ruth. He again refused to have anything to do with her. He wouldn't go near the bedroom or sit on her lap. We had to abandon use of the whistle. It took several days to calm him down. Even if I lip-whistled he got upset and he was sure that it was Ruth who whistled.

Cats can become alcoholics just like humans. Some friends living in Greenwich Village, New York, had a cat named Gin. They had picked him up as a kitten in a nearby bar. He liked to drink the cream left in the bottom of glasses Alexanders had been served in. Of course there was some gin left in the cream and he got to like it. He would become quite tipsy and hilarious to watch. Our friends took him home and helped him kick the habit by giving him spots of cream without the gin.

Experiments in alcoholism have used cats. To me it's a typical use and abuse of the feline to prove the obvious. Dr. Jules Masserman, professor and co-chairman of the Department of Psychiatry at Northwestern University, ran through an elaborate test with a cat to prove that "psychopathic states arise when an organism is faced with an unresolved tension—when it faces the choice of two modes of action neither of which is acceptable." The laboratory cat learned a series of maneuvers to get fish cakes from a box. After it had mastered this routine, the test was changed so that the cat got a blast of cold air when it opened the box to get the fish cakes. Then apparently it was allowed to go hungry or face the blast of air, accept an unacceptable situation or starve, an equally unacceptable situation. At this point the cat was offered the choice of milk or a mixture of milk and alcohol. It chose the latter, and under the influence of booze opened the box, completely disregarding the blast of air and got the fish cake. However, then it became a "miserable, slovenly, sick cat."

Of course! What did the experimenters expect? When they showed the cat kindness and no blast of air, it regained its normal self-esteem, chose milk, and resumed what the reporter called "living the good life." There is nothing in the entire experiment that any halfway intelligent person couldn't foretell. It is an example of the "games" scientists play to make their jobs seem important, to get money from the government and other sources of scientific grants.

For people who are convinced that Man is a superior being and has the right to use non-human animals for any purpose, it is amusing and no doubt convincing proof of the greatness of science. Few people reading an account of this experiment will raise any question as to its validity. Too many people feel that the scientist is infallible. As Dr. Michael Fox said when interviewed by Ms. Emily Hahn for the *New Yorker Magazine*, "In the great scientific brush off— knowledge for knowledge's sake—the justification for all kinds of inane work in science, the scientist simply hasn't assessed what he is doing in relation to global priorities."

Just ordinary happenings in an environment can produce some unusual feline attitudes. While still living in Putnam, New York, I saw Leo Quintus conditioned to be fearless of dogs by a simple fortuitous incident.

That September my first novel was published and we had a party. A car load of friends came down from Poughkeepsie and with them a Scotty dog. Ruth and I went out to greet our guests and Leo IV, as always, went along as part of the welcoming party. I don't know where Quin was at the time.

When the Scotty got out of the car, Leo IV took off around the house. Seeing a cat running, the Scotty naturally took after him. Then Quin appeared from somewhere and took after the dog. Leo found sanctuary up the cat ladder and into our bedroom. The Scotty was called and we went into the house, dog included.

During the eating, drinking and talking, I didn't pay attention to dog and cat. As the evening progressed I suddenly realized that Quin was parading grandly among our guests, socializing, while the Scotty hid beneath the couch.

As Quin moved from one person to another, accepting attention offered, he kept one eye on the couch. If the dog tried to come out, Quin edged over toward him, made a quick pass and the Scotty took cover again. Before the evening was over, all he had to do was look toward the dog to make him retire. And all of this was apparently because he thought he had chased the dog around the house, when the dog had really been chasing his older brother Leo.

After that conditioning Quin feared no dog. A neighbor had a mean Airedale that would attack a cat on sight. Once he came up to our place and jumped Quin. To the dog's surprise, Quin clawed him savagely across the nose. He never bothered Quin again.

Another time a pair of dachshunds attacked Quin. I rushed out to see what all the yelping was about. Quin crouched in the center of a circle of two yelping dogs. His eyes were intent with excitement. It was like an animal bevatron. Each time a dog passed in front of him he raked it with his claws, making it go faster and yelp louder. I had to rescue the two dogs before he wore them out.

Actually he became fearless of cars as well as dogs and people. This fearlessness may have been partially responsible for his death a couple of years later.

A small change in an environment may alter considerably the behavior of cats. In 1959 I began the building of our present home here in the Valley of the Moon. It's only about 300 yards higher on the ridge above our first house.

When the new house was almost finished and the other one sold, I began moving our belongings up in a borrowed pickup truck. Every time I went up to the house to work I took a load. This went on for several days. As the pieces of familiar furniture disappeared from where we lived, the cats became restless. When Ruth brought them up to the new house they sniffed out each item in its new location. I expected them to recognize each piece even if they didn't quite understand what was happening.

Charles seemed the most disturbed as the rooms of the home he was familiar with emptied. He'd come in to eat, then hurry out. Sometimes he joined the other cats on their afternoon strolls with Ruth and sometimes not.

Tang stuck close to Ruth or me. The last time anything like this had happened in his life was six or seven years earlier when his original household had broken up and he was given to us. Maybe he feared being given away again. If he had been a greedy cat it would have been easy to say that he was only staying close to the food source. But he was a choosey eater and such an explanation wouldn't hold up. Also he might have been afraid that his family would disappear and he would be abandoned.

Topsy, although older, always stayed close to Tang.

It took all of the final day to finish our moving. Ruth, Tang and Topsy walked up in the early dusk. The cats examined the new place as they had every day, checking out sleep spots, locating their food dishes. They ate, settled down and washed. They seemed completely at home.

Charles hadn't been around all day, and didn't come when Ruth called him before she and the other two cats walked up. On my last trip, I found him in the other house obviously hungry and hoping for his supper but his dishes were gone. The empty rooms terrified him. I closed the flexport so that he couldn't get out. Then I got the cat-carrier and opened it on the kitchen floor. He panicked. Talking, coaxing and closing doors, I finally cornered him, caught him and deposited him in the carrier. He let out a horrible yowl as I carried him out to the truck. All the way up to the new house he howled on the seat beside me while I talked and tried to calm him. When I drove into the carport he was still going full blast. I took the carrier into the kitchen. The Siamese were hysterical, creeping about in terror, hair bristling. Setting the carrier in front of the cats' dishes, I tilted back the top. Charles let out one last wail, rose up, became silent, looked around, saw the familiar dishes, jumped out and began to eat.

I took the carrier away. The Siamese came cautiously up and sniffed Charles. He paid no attention to them until he finished eating, then he acknowledged their sniffs with a sniff of his own. Who knows what he said to them.

With a slight toss of his big head, he swaggered into the family room and checked up on the furniture. He made himself completely at home. Thereafter, he came and went as if he had always lived in this new house. He still hunted in his old haunts down the ridge but he came up to the new house to eat and sleep.

It was the transformation in Tang and Topsy that surprised us. The Siamese had always treated Charlie as the barncat he was, while they were nobility. Tang liked to hassle him and intimidate him. Topsy had been responsible for injuring him as a kitten. Now she snubbed him. However, after the incident of the moving, they treated him with great respect. It was weeks before Tang hassled him again, and then it was more in play than "put-down."

We always said it was the ride in the truck that gave the black-and-white "one-up" on the Siamese. "You guys had to walk," he might have told them. "But I rode up in style." Then maybe it was the furious yowling that he was making on arrival that put the fear of the cat-god into them. Whichever, either or both, that environmental change brought about new behavior in our cat family.

4

When Your Cat Talks Do You Listen?

We have always talked to our cats from the time they arrived in our family as kittens or adult cats. This fits biologists Hubel's and Wiesel's suggested routine to enhance their "linguistic ability." And we use a "wide spectrum of language," but I'm not sure that it accomplishes anything. Our cats all make sounds which I find difficult to tie to meaning and am unable to pronounce.

The dictionary lists the following echoic pronunciation of sounds a cat makes: *Meow, Meou, Miaow, Mew, Miaou.* Some books about cats list *Mau* and *Mineow.*

Apparently over the years of association with cats, Man has fitted what he thinks he hears them say into stereotype echoic words. If you listen carefully to what a cat says you will soon see that few if any sounds they make will fit the above spellings. Some authorities have claimed that the cat makes upward of 100 different sounds, which places feline language along with Chinese.

I'm not suggesting that the cat is trying to imitate human speech. But it is possible that what he says has meaning that applies to certain situations, conditions, desires, or perhaps a number of wants. We make sounds at them. They make sounds back at us. They seem to understand some of the sounds we make.

The first time I consciously tried to spell what a cat said was when I thought Tang had asked me, through the window on the deck, to let him in. Sometimes he would just sit and look at me like the time I tried communication by pointing my finger. This time when our eyes met, he said, "Uhwow," or Oowow." That's my echoic spelling. He only said it once. I went to the sliding glass door and opened it. He came in and behaved as if I had reacted the way he expected me to.

He could have used the flexport but that was halfway around the house. Of course anyone who lives with cats knows that if a human is present to serve them, they expect service. If Ruth had come up on the deck and the glass door had been locked she would have asked me to open it for her when she might have gone to another door that was open. I'd have let her in too.

Sometimes our cats use "body language" to be let out or in. Mao paces around restlessly until I notice and open the door for him. If I ignore him he'll go out the flexport on his own.

There are times when I can appreciate a cat's reluctance to use the flexport. When Curley's deformed ear became infected after a fight, the pressure of the plastic leaves hurt it. Since that time he scratches at the flexport to let me know that he wants me to let him through the people's door.

However, if a heavy woman visits us, nothing can stop Curley from going through that flexport. Ruth insists that a fat woman reminds him of the person who moved into the place where he had been left behind and made his life miserable until he found us. But that has to do with conditioning and not language.

Yet even flight can be a form of communication. It's

respected by wildlife in the wilderness. Not long ago I called upon a neighbor, a young woman with cats, who lived in rather make-shift quarters while her house was being built. I came upon her suddenly, and thinking I had startled her, I apologized. Her casual reply was, "Oh, I knew someone was coming when my cats took off."

Recently Ruth and I spent an evening at a friend's house. She had just returned from a European trip and showed us a collection of slides. When she hung a sheet from the molding at one end of the room for a picture screen, it necessitated the moving of the chair her cat Sasha slept in. After the viewing, we settled back to talk about her trip and sip Drambuie. The chair had not been replaced. Sasha had been in and out all evening. Once she got up on our friend's lap but didn't stay long. She went to the door opening onto the terrace and wanted out. I let her out, though I knew she had her own door. In a little while she was back in again. She went to where her chair was, hopped up into it and down again almost immediately.

To anyone watching, she was communicating very well. I put the chair where it belonged and the carpet guards under each leg. Before I finished Sasha was in the chair preparing to nap.

That is not a new story to anyone who lives with a cat or cats. I observed and responded to Sasha's wishes. There was nothing new or unusual about what I did, except that I treated Sasha as a "people."

Another time a cat talked directly to me. We were visiting a place for the first time and I sat in a chair in the living room. I had hardly settled down before a big grey, neutered cat came into the room, placed himself in front of me and began mouthing a variety of feline sounds.

Our hostess said, "Don't pay any attention to him. You're just sitting in his chair."

I moved to another and apologized to him for occupying his seat. He promptly took the one I had vacated.

When people come to our house, they very often ask if they're taking my chair before they sit down. If for some reason it was necessary for me to sit in a particular chair, I'd say so and suggest they take another. All of which is only normal consideration and courtesy among humans. In the above incident I only had to understand common relationships between people to understand what the cat wanted. But St. George Jackson Mivart, well-known English scientist, said, "We cannot, without becoming cats, perfectly understand the cat mind."

Of course that's true—to a degree—but it is almost equally true for understanding the mind of another person. To "perfectly understand" someone else we would have to be that someone. The minds of humans are near enough alike to make it possible for two or more people to approach mentally on a similar level. Assuming that all mammalian brains function similarly, perhaps we can, with an effort, understand the feline mind. Of course, this is treating cats (or all mammals) as equals, as having rights and privileges the same as humans. I'm sure that many people, especially scientists, will say that this only proves that I am being anthropomorphic. However, in the incidents cited above, my behavior and the cat's behavior coincided.

A few years ago an editorial in *CATS Magazine* stated: "Eccentricities of cat behavior are frequently mentioned in major publications as cats swim, make cross-country trips alone, adopt dogs, birds, etc., and generally act contrary to the normal, accepted routines. Frequently the stylized patterns which our domesticated animals adopt seem to be extensions of our own behavior. The anthropomorphic characteristics we see in our pets have frequently been derided by behavioral scientists who tell us that the structured tendencies in the actions of 'lower' animals are simply reactions to environmental stimuli in relation to the domestic situation and its restrictions, and that any related reaction is coincidental."

That's how the "behavioral scientists" see it. Yet I must ask: how does the behavior of a normal human reacting "to environmental stimuli in relation to the domestic situation and its restrictions," differ from that of the "lower" animals?

I can see only one difference: the "lower" animal, in this case the cat, can't put the relationship or problem into words.

Perhaps if non-human animals could talk to us in English about a situation, the behavioral scientists wouldn't consider a human acceptance of their reactions as anthropomorphic.

A couple of years ago, Ruth was in the local hospital with a back injury. One of her nurses told her that she liked cats and that she probably wouldn't be alive if it hadn't been for the family cat. She said that she was upstairs, an infant in her crib, and her mother was downstairs reading. The cat came down crying and carrying on, but the mother paid no attention to him, assuming that he just wanted to be fed.

Then the cat attacked her, scratching her ankles. That got her attention. She jumped up to punish the cat but the animal raced up the stairs, looking back. The mother followed and found her baby, the present nurse, face down in her crib smothering.

Perhaps this "unrelated reaction" to an "environmental stimuli" as the behavioral scientists put it "is coincidental." But it was a happy coincidence, wouldn't you say?

Another incident: When the house of a deaf woman was on fire, her cat began jumping up and down on the woman's chest and kept screaming. The cat's screaming went unheard, but it communicated its message to its mistress without words.

The behavioral scientists shrug off such accounts because they can't be repeated in a laboratory. Now if one cat had been able to say, "Hey, lady, your kid is suffocating," and the other had been able to say in sign language, "Hey, lady, your house is on fire," that would have put them right up there with human animals. No laboratory repetition would be necessary to convince the hardnosed scientists that your cat shouldn't be ignored when it tries to communicate.

If "cleanliness is next to godliness" then the cat is right up there several ladder rungs ahead of Man. No cat is unclean that is given the proper chance in its "domestic situation" to be clean. If it has the opportunity to go out doors and do its privy a cat will always go out, sometimes in very inclement weather. If given the use of a litter box, it will use it. If a cat gets out of line the fault lies almost always with the human.

Fifty years ago, before the days of commercial cat litter, when torn up newspaper was used for a cat's privy pan in a city apartment, we had trouble getting our first Leo to change from country dirt to city newspaper. We didn't recognize the fact that a cat conditioned to one finds it hard to change abruptly to the other.

We had no trouble with Leo once we learned that a little dirt mixed with the litter helped him make the change. But changing a cat's toilet pan, especially back in the days of strips of paper, was a disagreeable chore. I put off doing it as long as possible, sometimes too long.

One evening as Ruth and I were reading, Leo began scratching the rug in the center of the room. When he drew our attention he squatted over the spot. I yelled at him and he dived beneath the couch. I dragged him out and took him to his pan. It smelled pretty high, but there were still some dry scraps of paper. I showed him them. He went through an elaborate covering up routine on the floor beside the pan, then went back to his sanctuary beneath the couch.

Was more communication necessary? I changed the paper. He used the new litter. Maybe he didn't know what he was doing, but he did get the message across. "I don't want to break protocol, but I'm not going to use that stinking litter pan until it's changed."

A few years later, after Leo Tertius was left alone and no red tabby kittens were available as a companion for him, we took in a cat boarder. It was a red tabby, one of Tersh's younger brothers who had spent the winter in the city. His name was Orpheus, called Orphy.

Orphy was conditioned to using torn up newspapers in a pan. He simply wouldn't go outdoors to do his privy. When I showed him nice, soft dirt, he would do nothing and immediately go back to the house and want in. He didn't do anything in the house either—I mean he didn't "go" on the floor or rug. Like his father in the city apartment, confronted with scraps of paper instead of dirt, he just held it.

I even tried to get the message through to him with a spanking but that didn't work and he showed no resentment of my chastisement. He didn't run away or hide from me. Maybe he sensed that his sort of passive-resistance would get the message to me in the end. It did. I fixed some torn up newspapers for him. He used the pile enthusiastically. But when I came to preparing a fresh box, I dumped the used lot in the birch grove and only partly covered it with dirt. I showed Orphy the spot. After a few repetitions and much explanation each time, which I'm sure most people would consider meaningless, he understood what I had been trying to get him to do. In no time he quit using torn paper and returned to using dirt, going and coming via the ladder and the window like his older brother Tersh.

Sometimes communication with our cats about toilet gets a bit personal. In August of that same year, Orphy's owner came and took him back to the city. By this time Mother Penny's late litter of red tabby kittens were, we thought, old enough for us to take one as a companion for Tersh. He became Leo IV, or just plain Leo again.

He was an agreeable, good-natured youngster and Tersh, his older half-brother, accepted him quickly. However, he may have been taken away from Penny before she was through with her training. He had a trick which Ruth didn't find particularly flattering. It appeared that he transferred his mother-image to her.

There was no problem about him doing his privy outdoors and covering it properly. But he still seemed to expect his mother to clean him up. After a trip to the woods, he'd ask to be let into the house again. If Ruth happened to be sitting or reclining on the couch, he would climb on her chest and turn his rear end up to her face. There was no doubt in her mind about what he meant. After a light swat or two and admonition to do his own cleanup, he got over this little quirk and became as fastidious as any of our cats.

We seldom had any communication problem with our cats when it came to taking walks. They were willing to go several days in succession along the ridge in our "south forty," or into the ravine in the "east forty." But sometimes they would decide which trip they wanted to take and if we didn't heed them, they might go along on the one chosen, but they'd make known their displeasure by sulking.

Tang, the Siamese, was the most demanding about having his own way. But he would become very frustrated if we didn't go on a walk at all. If Ruth didn't take him on a walk when he expected her to, he would eat the laces out of her sneakers. Several new sets of laces later she understood his message.

Even when we do listen to our cats the communication barrier is insurmountable. Mabel, an elderly widow, rented the apartment on the lower level of our present house. She liked cats. She liked Tang and he was in the habit of visiting her. When he felt like it he would go down and she would open the sliding glass door or screen for him to come in. He talked to her a lot and she talked to him. We could hear this murmur of conversation going on downstairs.

Mabel let Tang have privileges he didn't have with us.. He walked on counters, slept in her bed, received scraps of fresh chicken. This in no way alienated his relationship with us; we were his people, our home was his home. Mabel was just a good friend whom he visited when she was home and he felt like it but she had to let him in. Upstairs he had a flexport. He could go and come and didn't have to bother us—unless, of course, he felt like getting a little people-service.

Above the counter and sink at the kitchen end of the apartment a strip of windows overlooked the valley. Just outside were a couple of sizable live oak trees in a large outcropping of lava rock. If Mabel was working at that end of the kitchen, and Tang wanted to come in for a visit, he would sit on one of those boulders and call to her. She let him in through a sliding door opening on the terrace and he would come around and enter.

One time when she let him in, he followed her back into the kitchen, got up on the counter by the window facing the lava rock he'd been sitting on and began talking to her. She asked him what he wanted, offered him food, which he refused. He got down from the counter and went to the door to get out. She opened it for him. When she returned to the kitchen, he was back on the boulder again. The window sash was pushed back and he talked to her through the screen. Mabel asked him if he wanted back in and went around to the terrace door. He appeared outside and she let him in. Again he followed her into the kitchen, got up on the counter in front of the window screen and began talking.

Now Mabel was fed up with his behavior. She started to scold him. Then it occurred to her that he was talking about something. But what? She thought about it for a while, then speculated that he might be telling her that if she had a flexport, like the one upstairs, put in that screen, he could go and come without making her so much trouble. It would be more convenient for them both. She explained to him that she couldn't put a flexport in that screen. He would have to take the problem up with the landlord—me. Tang continued arguing with her and she repeated her explanation. Finally he gave up and went hunting. That ended the matter. Mabel thought it was a great joke.

It is easy for skeptics to point out that Mabel's little scenario is a typical example of anthropomorphism. And they will be quite right—as far as the human knowledge takes it. Tang was certainly concerned or disturbed about something. If humans are the superior animals they pretend to be, they should be able to crack the feline language code. Then Mabel might have found out what was really bugging that Siamese.

Perhaps, to paraphrase Hamlet, "There are more things in a cat's personality, *behavioral scientists*, than are dreamed of in your philosophy."

Some Notes on Feline Personality

5

It's natural to clutch at any and all incidents that can be interpreted to support one's beliefs. Scientists, no matter what branch of science, are as guilty as anyone else—especially when they get out of their familiar field. In my observations of cat behavior and the conclusions drawn I'm well aware of the possibility of misinterpretation simply because I'm fond of cats.

When our second Leo, Sec, was recovering from a long bout in the hospital, an orange-yellow tabby tom showed up in the neighborhood with one front foot missing. We called him "Three Legs"—not a spectacularly original name, but one that came naturally and fit. I had no idea whose cat he was. We felt sure he was one of our first Leo's progeny—a half brother of Sec. He had apparently been caught in a trap and had gnawed himself free. Sec and he used to quarrel over territory. Because of their respective handicaps they were fairly evenly matched and I felt that their quarreling was more therapeutic than dangerous.

Once when they were sparring at the end of our cottage, I decided to stop the encounter. My appearance distracted Three Legs and Sec rushed him. Sec's wobbly charge caused by his back injury unnerved most adversaries. But this time the two tangled, growling, snarling and chewing, then broke apart. In this pause, Tersh, our first neutered cat, bounded out of the birch grove, sailed over the two combatants and landed several feet away. His eyes were wild with excitement. This was a great game. He wasn't mad at anyone.

That ended the fight. Sec drew back. Three Legs disappeared around the house. And Tersh came to me, tail whipping, eyes flashing, perhaps saying in good solid cat language, "Man! That was real fun!"

That was the last I saw of Three Legs. He probably met the unhappy end of unneutered toms—especially one so handicapped.

Some years later I thought about him when I read Karl A. Menninger's book, *Man Against Himself*, and came upon this passage: "When a weasel or mink gnaws off its own leg to escape a trap, it does so, so far as we can judge, consciously and deliberately and accepts, so to speak, the full responsibility of the self-preservative self-destruction."

Dr. Menninger fell into an anthropomorphic trap. I can assure you that weasels and minks are not the only animals who gnaw off their legs to gain freedom from traps. I have known rabbits to do it. In no case could it or would it have been done consciously and deliberately.

When a non-human animal is caught in a steel trap, the first sensation must be pain and fear; panic follows. The animal pulls frantically to get free. He turns, twists, bites at the steel, continuing to struggle until he approaches exhaustion.

The grip of the trap jaws gradually cuts the circulation in the trapped leg. Finally the animal stops to rest and finds the pain gone. Yet he is still held. He bites at the trap. He bites at this dead thing held in the trap. He begins to gnaw. As soon as his teeth reach flesh with feeling, he stops gnawing and resumes struggling. Such action deadens the flesh farther along the trapped limb and allows him to gnaw some more.

There is nothing conscious or deliberate about any of this. There is no reason to assume that this animal knows this thing he is gnawing at is a part of his own body until his teeth bite into a part of his flesh that has feeling. Unless, of course, we're willing to assume that this non-human animal's consciousness has evolved as far as a human's. No, when he feels pain, he stops gnawing and starts throwing himself about again. Finally the bones are bare. In one of his lunges, they snap off and he is free—free but minus a leg. That's probably how it happened with Three Legs.

There could be a connection between the behavior of a non-human animal chewing itself free from a trap and a human animal bent upon self-destruction. This relationship is real and important, and in a sense fits Dr. Menninger's theory of conscious and deliberate self-destruction. Such a relationship is based on the similarity of mammalian brains, not on the same levels of consciousness.

The human animal behaves in a more complicated way than the non-human animal largely because his frames of reference are more complicated. In either instance no self-destruction is deliberate. No suicide really commits the final act until some "trap," perhaps like some state of desperation deadens all the feeling he has in this thing, this self he is destroying.

Like any person, every cat has his own personality. Some traits are thrust upon him by circumstances. There's the case of Fat Albert who became a blood donor at a New Jersey Animal Hospital. He arrived there an abandoned and uncared-for pet. Dr. Gloria Weintraub didn't have the heart to euthanize him and after she had fixed up his abscessed ear and rid him of the parasites that plagued him, she discovered he was quite willing to give blood for other pets as if he enjoyed it. He became a special fixture at the hospital.

The University of Oregon's Health Sciences Center has

been researching *tinnitus*. It is a ringing in the ears and because it develops gradually, people haven't the faintest idea of when the condition starts. Many things have been found to affect the degree of ringing, but no cure. A most unique example of the malady was found in a cat named Zinger who belongs to a campus receptionist.

When word of this research project came to the attention of the receptionist, she brought Zinger into the lab. The researchers made a recording of the tone—4000 hertz—a very pure tone that never wavered. However, the receptionist wouldn't let the researchers use her cat for experimentation. She did promise them a kitten if Zinger ever had a litter. That seemed a doubtful prospect because the loud ringing in Zinger's ears frightened tomcats away.

There's a Siamese cat here in the Valley of the Moon who likes to swim in the family swimming pool. That's a trait not too common among cats. Perhaps the only reason this one likes it is the reward: being dried by a thick towel afterward.

Our cats have all had their share of personality quirks. When Ruth and I lived in our first cottage in New York State, our dining table stood by a strip window that overlooked a rocky, brush-grown drainage area on that side of the house. Normally I sat at one end of the table and Ruth sat at the side facing the strip windows directly. When she went into the city for a couple of days I sat in her chair.

Our dining chairs had slightly curved backs. They didn't have to be pulled out from the table much to permit a cat to sit on the seat with his head above the table top. So when I ate it was common for Sec to sit at one end of the table and Tersh at the other. They watched each fork or spoonful of food as it traveled from my plate to my mouth. They swallowed ever so slightly when I swallowed.

At first I thought they watched because they were hungry and after sitting, feeling rather like a bloated plutocrat eating truffles while starving urchins looked on, I would get up and fix them some food. They weren't really hungry. They'd have a go at the food I fixed them—doing me a favor, you know—then back they'd come to eater-watching again.

I wish I knew why my eating fascinated them so much. Maybe they thought my table manners were terrible.

Those were the days before much canned catfood was on the market and it was Depression time so the cats ate pretty much what we ate. Most of our cats have eaten spaghetti with meat sauce.

The local barber gave Ruth some hot Italian peppers and she decided to cook them. As the water came to a boil, both Sec and Tersh rushed to the window and demanded out. Shortly afterwards our eyes began to smart and our noses to sting as they do in an L.A. smog. The pan of steaming peppers was hastily set outdoors. The message had reached our cats at least ten minutes before it got to us.

In modest amounts those peppers made fine flavoring for spaghetti sauce and Sec especially liked spaghetti. Once Ruth put a little more of the hot stuff in than usual but that didn't stop Sec. He ate a few bites, then turned to his milk dish and lapped milk furiously, then back again to the spaghetti.

At that time, baked beans were a Saturday night regularity in our home. Sec also liked baked beans. They behaved with him just as they do with most people. However, Sec tried to catch each explosion. The result was a wild pinwheel-like performance around the living room that pushed us close to hysteria.

Out here in California, Tiki, our first Siamese, who came from a household of cat thieves, grew into a big, tough hunter. He was neutered but still roamed a wide area. The family of my partner in writing "how-to" articles lived beyond the shop-office-studio complex where we worked. Tiki included their place in his territory. The family had two Siamese cats but it made no difference to Tiki. He let them know who was cat boss in the neighborhood and continued his regular patrolling. They never challenged him.

Our cats don't steal—at least not from us. And Tiki, in spite of his early environment, had been indoctrinated into cat rules at our place by our red tabby, Tim. However, one Sunday evening Ruth, Anne and I were in the patio of our first home out here. From where I sat, I could see down the driveway to the sharp turn that took it past my partner's home. Here came Tiki around that curve carrying something, head held high so that whatever it was wouldn't drag in the dirt. At first I thought he had made some special catch. As he came near, I saw that it *was* a special catch, the T-bone of a steak and there was still a lot of meat on it. Had he stolen it from our neighbors, off their barbecue fire, or from their own Siamese, or even their big Labrador retriever?

If they hadn't seen him do it, they might have suspected their dog of the theft when they noticed the disappearance of the bone; their dog would steal. I never mentioned the incident to the family and they never mentioned it to me.

Another time, Tiki caught a half-grown jack rabbit. He ate it on our small patch of lawn. It was much more than he could consume at one feeding. Age was showing on Timmy; most of his teeth were gone and he couldn't share the meal. After Tiki gorged himself he went to sleep on the lawn beside his catch. When he got hungry again he ate more rabbit. On the third day he apparently decided to get some exercise and took a walk.

By then the rabbit was smelling pretty high. I assumed that Tiki had all he wanted, so I took the remains and threw them into the woods behind us. I figured that the neighbor's dog on that side would find what was left of the rabbit and finish it off.

The next day, the partially gnawed carcass was back on the lawn with Tiki on guard over it. I talked him out of the well-chewed bones and buried them. They had become carrion to me, but to Tiki the remains were just "left-overs."

Cats have strange eating habits just as people have. A friend of ours had a cat who loved popcorn. When she brought a bag home he would tear it open and gobble up as much as he could hold. Our friend began rationing the popped kernels a handful at a time. The cat gobbled the first handful and asked for more. No more was forthcoming.

After a few such rejections his attitude changed. When the handful of white kernels was placed on the floor, he approached them and sniffed them over carefully. Then he separated one popped kernel from the pile with his paw, patted it gently across the room three or four feet and ate it to the last crumb. He went back and separated another kernel and repeated the routine. He did this until all of the daily ration was gone.

Our friend concluded that he was making this popcorn treat last as long as possible now that he could no longer stuff himself as he once could. He was "reacting to environmental stimuli and restrictions," just like some kid making his candy ration last as long as possible.

Tripe, which is the stomach lining of cattle, is not uncommon food for people. Many feline species eat the stomachs of their catches. Their prey are usually herbivores so they get vitamins that way.

Our Siamese, Tang, never ate the stomachs of mice, rats or gophers. I've known other cats to leave the part of an animal's liver that contains the bile sack. We have always called this practice "sorting." When we moved up to our second house here in California we found the area around it heavily populated with rodents. Every morning we made what we called a "stomach count" to see how the war on rodents went while we slept. The only other way we could have protected ourselves from such destructive enemies would have been by trap and poison. Our cats were fulfilling their ecological job as best they could.

No kid can reject spinach with more disdain than a cat can show when it chooses not to eat the choice catfood you've put down for it. You think you've offered it a respectable meal—oh, it was one of the cheaper brands, but . . . your cat sniffs the stuff, then makes scratching motions all around the dish as if it were excrement he wanted to bury.

There are different angles to this burying routine. Wild felines, specifically the mountain lion, bury what they don't eat of a catch. It's their way of putting leftovers in the frig. Wildlife specialists think this is done to keep other carnivores from stealing the remains.

In the feud between our Missy Manx and Burmese Benji, unless I could get her into our bedroom-bathroom area, I had to feed her in the patio or beyond the patio fence to avoid a battle. When I fed her outside the patio where there were leaves and dirt, she ate her fill, then buried what remained.

I never left her buryings to see if she would come back to them later, because besides our own cats around, there were other animals, dogs, strange cats and skunks. So I don't know if what she did revealed some atavistic trait or not. Or whether, after she had eaten her fill, she was merely registering a repugnance for what was left after her appetite was satisfied.

Cats do have other atavistic traits. Perhaps it's to show affection, or payment for food and shelter, or just a reflex action like a baby holding out a toy for an adult to take. All of our young cats have brought us presents. They start with small objects like leaves or stones. When they get older they offer us their catches. I don't think they expect us to eat such gifts; our praise and thanks is sufficient. We praise them lavishly when they catch something we want them to catch and show disapproval if it's something we don't want them to catch.

Young cats may even offer presents intended as jokes. Our Siamese, Mao, brought us presents before he did any serious hunting. Once he came in with a shiny, dried horse turd. He placed it on the carpet near Ruth, then withdrew a few feet, lay on his brisket, and looked from it to her and back. Was there a twinkle in his eyes? She had a feeling that he was playing a joke on her. It's hard to believe a cat can be scatologically minded; it does make one wonder.

Embarrassment is a feeling everyone has known at sometime and I would have thought that the subject had been thoroughly covered for non-humans. Yet when columnist Jack Smith stated, "no one has ever seen an embarrassed cat," his volume of mail jumped with ancedotes about embarrassed cats. Many of the letters were about cats misjudging a jump, falling short, looking ridiculous and being laughed at by humans.

One eighteen-pound tomcat tried to leap from the dining table to the buffet and missed. "Of course, we all laughed," the woman wrote. "He laid back his ears and, keeping his body as close to the floor as possible, raced out of the room and headed upstairs. That was an embarrassed cat!"

Did raucous laughter put this tomcat to flight, or did he feel ridiculed for his miscalculated jump? Our Leo IV would do tricks for laughs and our laughter didn't embarrass him. If he were showing off and goofed, our laughter would send him walking off indignantly.

If instead of laughing, I sympathize and say, "Oh, that's too bad. Poor Mao, or poor Curley, or poor so-and-so," there is no show of embarrassment or chagrin. Their reaction is the same as a people reaction.

Another woman wrote Columnist Smith about her Persian cat that had to be shaved because of matting. "He was no sooner back in the house than he caught sight of himself in a full-length mirror on a closet door. Believe me, that cat was embarrassed! Totally mortified! In fact he hid under my bed and came out only after dark to eat."

That seems to me to be a show of humiliation rather than embarrassment. That too is a feeling within the scope of the mammalian brain—human and non-human. I once knew an aggressive, blustering collie who became a cringing cur after he had been shaved, due to matting and the summer heat. He had been allowed to keep a ruff of long hair around his head and neck. It gave him the appearance of a lion, but his frame of reference didn't include the king of beasts so the tonsorial concession didn't help his morale.

Columnist Smith seemed to feel that the subject of feline embarrassment had been "already explored about as deeply as laymen could explore it, and that further inquiry ought to be left to the laboratory." Mr. Smith doesn't seem to understand either cats or "scientific laboratories." There is no way that the subject can be explored in the "rat psychologist's" milieu. The reason might be considered evidence of people difference. A cat just wouldn't see any sense in making a fool of himself for the benefit of the "scientific method."

The show of embarrassment can even be extended to birds, non-mammals. Here on the California coast I once watched a grey pelican fishing close on shore in a moderately rough surf. He tried to take flight. Three times as he was about to be airborne, a wave caught him and rolled him over and over. Each time he righted himself and came back to try again. After the third try, he gave up and swam toward open water with a show of dignity, as if saying, "The hell with it! I didn't intend to take off anyhow."

I had watched it all through binoculars and as the pelican swam away, he turned his head from side to side, watching me as if he knew I had seen his humiliating show. Maybe his whole performance with me watching meant nothing to him but if the biologist's information about the magnification of a bird's eyes is true, that pelican probably saw me better than I saw him. And maybe he thought that the human on the shore holding a black object to his face was only some distant threat. He might also have been saying to himself, in pelicanese, "I wonder if that damn fool human is going to laugh?"

It was the French philosopher Montaigne who wrote, "When my cat and I entertain each other with mutual apish tricks, as playing with a garter, who knows but I make my cat more sport than she makes me? And who knows but that she pities me for being no wiser than to play with her?" Monsieur Montaigne recognized a people-to-people relationship with his cat companion.

Our Siamese, Sci-Fi, Si for short, was a cat that had a pronounced sense of fun and games. As he grew from kittenhood he developed a strange manner of walking; he lapped one front leg across in front of the other at each step. This brought to mind the cross-gartered effect of Shakespeare's Malvolio, and we called him Malvolio at times.

When he felt especially cocky about something he held his

tail so straight up that it seemed to lift his hind feet off the ground. His way of showing exuberance was to bring his long tail up over his back scorpion-like, tapping the tip of it on his spine. We called him "Scorpy" at times.

He liked to get up on Ruth's chest and do an elaborate job of smooching, ending up by putting his nose under her chin.

When he got on my lap, and just wanted to lie down, he never seemed to lower himself. Instead, he seemed to pull up his legs and drop all his weight.

Anne and George came for a visit. George began a game with Si, one he played with his own Siamese. He held his hands clawlike to threaten Si. Instead of being frightened, Si was fascinated. He'd race around the family room on short-legs, then jump upon the couch and hide his head beneath a cushion, play-acting terror.

After George left, I continued this game with Si. We usually played it at bedtime. Ruth would be reading, sitting on the couch with Si stretched out on her lap. The moment I began my bedtime preparations, up would come his head, ears alert. When I threatened him with claw-hands, he'd streak away. Over, around and under couch and chairs he'd go. Sometimes when he pretended to hide I would catch him up in my "claws" and pretend to bite him. He would open his mouth very wide, throwing back his head as if laughing. I've seen small children behave like this when someone pretended they were going to "eat them all up."

Then, as part of the game, Si would pretend to bite my finger and wrap his feet around my hands. He never used his claws and all the time he purred like crazy. If I stopped the game but didn't immediately go to bed, he'd come sailing from some hiding place, cavorting on short-legs in front of me, teasing for more game. He was as obviously fascinated by this terror-game as any human child would be.

When spring came and he grew older, he spent more time at night hunting. He usually got in by the time Ruth and I had our bedtime snack so he and I would have our little game.

One night he didn't return home until late. He was tired

and stretched out on Ruth's lap. When I made the motions to start the game, he gave me a look that said plainly enough, "Aw boss, do we have to play that silly game tonight? I'm bushed!" And I thought of Montaigne's remarks. Si and I didn't play that night.

Some cats are more sensitive than others. Our present red tabby, Curley, had a "thin skin" in spite of a tough early life.

One morning he pestered me at my desk about something. Maybe he wanted my lap for awhile; maybe he wanted my chair; maybe he just wanted to get some messages across to me. Anyhow, he was interfering with my work. First I scolded him, then I picked him up and put him out on the deck and closed the sliding door behind him with finality.

It was a foggy, grey, cold California morning. He stood looking back at me. Had he been a human, a person would have said that he had an injured look in his eyes. Then he walked along the deck and around the corner of the house.

Later a misty drizzle started, and feeling guilty about putting him out in the wet, I went looking for him. He had curled up in the leaves beneath one of the huge lava rocks down below the front side of the house. He was well-sheltered. I tried to coax him out. My morning's work done, I could give him some attention now but he refused to come to me. He didn't return to the house until evening.

Another time when he had been disciplined for some reason which he undoubtedly felt was unfair, I found him out in my shop on a piece of burlap. I remembered what the woman (who moved into the house where he had been abandoned) had said: "He sleeps on a piece of burlap down in the basement."

I picked him up and carried him into the house and he purred. I wondered what had gone on in his mind. Was he feeling sorry for himself? Did sleeping on that piece of burlap signify in his mind a return to the days when he had no family? How like a kid with injured feelings he had behaved! I remembered my own childhood when hurt feelings were accompanied by the words, "I'll go out in the garden and live on worms."

6

Sometimes You Have to Transport Cats

At the time we moved from Putnam County to the Valley of the Moon we had two cats, Leo IV and Timmy. I brooded for days over the problem of transporting them. I considered leaving them with the people who bought our New York State place, but even in my immature state of cat-consciousness at that time, I shied away from that sort of abandonment.

We bought our California property with some friends who were already out here. I considered shipping our cats by air and letting our friends pick them up and take care of them until we got there. Then I realized the problem of making the cats understand what we were doing to them. Care of our cats on a plane would be dubious—after all they were only "animals." Finally, I decided to take them with us: two adults, a five-year-old youngster, and two grown cats traveling 3,000 miles in a Chevy. There would be problems enough for three humans. Filling stations had "facilities" for people, and there were motels and homes—but as for cats?

Our cats did their privy outdoors; they were not used to a litterbox. Both of them were well past the age of learning new routines easily. We couldn't let them out of the car with any assurance they'd come back when we were ready to leave. They would not use the same litterbox, so I made one for each to fit on the floor in front of the back seat.

It was a two-door Chevy, so I made hardboard panels to fit the gaps between the front seat and the side of the doors so that the cats couldn't duck down and out when we stopped for any reason. But what about car trouble? Suppose the engine had to be worked on in a public garage? We had only one cat carrier. It wouldn't hold two cats. We might get a second, but the cats couldn't be kept in carriers for any great length of time.

So I built a trailer—something like a small luggage trailer. The problem was solved: a place to put our cats in the event of car trouble, or if we all grew tired of riding with each other in the car, or if our own sleeping accommodations wouldn't allow pets. I also bought harnesses for both of them.

We set out for California in the rain and seemed to travel most of way in the rain. Except for some complaining each morning when the cats thought they should get out and hunt, they traveled better than our five-year-old daughter. The trip took three weeks and there were only two cat-related bad experiences. At a motel in Ohio a strong smell of gas in the room disturbed both the cats and us. I couldn't find the cause and I hesitated to complain because of our "pets." Finally I decided to take Leo out for some air. I put his harness on him and carried him into the parking area. When I put him down, he walked right out of his harness. It was dark and relatively quiet, but chilly and misty damp. Leo was not about to take off back to Putnam County on such a night. I coaxed him from under the car and took him inside. By keeping two windows slightly open we were able to minimize the smell of gas fumes and get some sleep.

Then, on the way up the North Platte in Nebraska, we

stopped at a service station in a little town. We all went to the rest room. The cats were left in the car as usual. I got back first and Timmy was gone. The wing of the door on the driver's seat side was open just enough to let a small cat through. Leo sat comfortably on the back of the front seat. Panic! I pulled the car and trailer out into the street and parked it. When Ruth and Anne returned we began searching the neighborhood, calling. No Timmy. After half an hour of hunting, we gave up. The only thing we could do was run an ad in the local paper asking if someone found a lost red tabby to write us in California and we'd send what it cost to have him shipped to us. A very unhappy trio returned to the car, ready to look for the newspaper office. As I opened the door on the driver's side, Timmy crawled out from under the seat on the opposite side. The gloomy three became a very relieved and happy three.

Taking a cat to the vet has always been hard for me. When Charlie, the black-and-white, developed tooth trouble, I put off taking him as long as possible because he hated the carrier and riding in the car. Since he wasn't eating and was obviously in pain, I made the appointment, put him in the carrier and loaded up. He yowled loud enough for all the neighborhood to hear. Tang heard and knew that Charlie was being taken away.

As I drove along I explained to Charlie that the vet would fix his sore tooth and Charlie yowled louder. I hoped that my soothing tone would somehow convey to him my good intentions.

The vet found a decayed molar. He stuffed Charlie, a big cat, into a metal box. This device allowed the head, all four legs and the rear end to be exposed for examination. All edges were smooth and if the cat struggled he couldn't hurt himself.

Anyhow, the vet removed Charlie's bad tooth and Charlie screamed, spinning around in the confinement of the box. I talked to him, stroked his head, tried to calm him, feeling all the time that his hatred and fear of me mounted with every twinge of hurt.

We removed him from the box and put him in the carrier. When I started home he yowled louder than ever. I began talking to him again about going home to Ruth and Tang. He quieted. I wondered if the removal of the infected tooth had begun to make him feel more comfortable. If he felt better, perhaps I could do some shopping, save a special trip to the market. When I stopped at the store, he miowed with a rising inflection as if asking, "Are we home?" I explained about buying groceries, then we'd go on home. He didn't say any more until I started up again, and I assured him that we were on our way home this time.

Our mailbox is on Cavedale, a county road, one-quarter mile from our house. When I reached it I stopped to pick up our mail. Again Charlie asked, "Are we home?" I explained why I was stopping and that soon we'd be on our way again. We arrived; I carried him into the kitchen and opened the carrier by his dishes. I hoped that the sight of familiar things would soften his traumatic condition. I really expected him to leap out of the cage and flee in terror. Instead, he hopped out calmly, went to his dishes and began to eat. He looked around at Tang who came cautiously to sniff him, then resumed eating. Of course, he hadn't been able to eat for several days and he was hungry.

After that terrible experience, instead of showing fear or distrust of me, he treated me like a benefactor, a special friend. When he came into the house, he would march toward me. Head-on, his gait was something to watch, his shoulders rolled at each step and he looked as if he were tromping the floor with the weight of a bull. He'd come straight at me to butt his head against my leg, purring louder than I'd ever heard him before. I thought it might be food he wanted but it wasn't that. He was simply greeting me—greeting that big cat who had done something good for him once. Now, even outdoors where he at one time seemed afraid of me, he'd let me close enough to pet him.

Transporting cats across country or to the vet is traumatic enough, but transporting a cat or three cats under crisis conditions can be harrowing.

Early one September morning, gusty winds whipped pow-
erlines together on a back canyon road five miles up the
valley. Sparks on tinder-dry roadside vegetation started a
fire. It moved north, away from us, and for a time it
appeared that the fire crews would control it. Then around
two o'clock the following Monday morning, forty-eight
hours after the fire began, the wind shifted. The still
smoldering southern edge came to life and the fire started
toward us. It was still three miles away. The fire fighters
tried to control the flanks, but gusts of wind up to eighty
miles an hour swept the flames around or over any gains
they made. By Monday afternoon the front moved steadily
closer. From higher on our ridge, I stood and watched it
approach.

How was I to transport three cats, Topsy, Tang, and
Charlie, with only one cat carrier if we were forced to
evacuate? I couldn't put Charlie in with either of the
Siamese. Tang, I was sure, would rip a cardbord box apart.
Topsy might stay in one, terrified, possibly in a state of
shock. It never occurred to me to try borrowing extra
carriers. After all, we might not need them—I hoped.

Then I remembered a large wire cage behind our pumphouse. A friend had made it to trap a feral cat without
injuring it and I had stored the cage for him. I couldn't have
felt more relief if I had been told the fire was controlled.
Charles could go in the cat carrier; the two Siamese in the
cage. This solution made all other preparations for leaving, if
it came to that, seem simple.

Midnight passed before we were ordered to pull out. We
loaded a few things in a friend's station wagon. Special
papers and the cats we put in our car and drove out in the
thickening smoke.

Charlie, in the carrier, bellowed a protest occasionally.
Topsy huddled in the cage but said nothing. However, Tang
sat up alert, sometimes placing his front paws high on the
screen and filled the car with his fierce Siamese complaint.

We talked to him and tried to explain what was happening.
As we turned off the highway, which the fire seemed to be

following, the whipping flames revealed torching fence posts, and blazing skeletons of wooden structures on our right. In the rear window lights glared from cars forced to detour the approaching fire. We drove across the valley between solid lines of parked sightseers' cars.

This must have seemed wild and threatening to Tang. Yet I didn't feel he was screaming in panic. He knew what flames were, what a fire was. He loved a fire in the fireplace. He was yelling for an explanation: "For crissakes tell us what's going on!"

Here we were, two "superior" human animals, priding ourselves on being relatively intelligent and we couldn't explain the situation to him in his own language.

We followed our friend in the station wagon to his home on the other side of the valley. I put the cats in a guest cabin, the cat carrier with its screen window against the cage so the three cats could sniff noses as well as see each other.

Every half hour or so I looked in on them, talked to them, trying to reassure. Topsy and Charlie were bellied down, paws tucked beneath. Tang no longer complained or demanded explanation. He sat erect, alert. Each time I visited them he met me with a look that seemed to me to ask: "What does it mean?"

The main fire front had moved into the Hooker Creek Canyon. I drove over to find out if we still had a house. A forestry official advised me to get back into our house as soon as possible to prevent any possibility of looting and to watch for flair-ups of spot fires. I drove back to get Ruth and the cats.

On our return we found a patrolman stationed at the intersection of the road across the valley and the highway north of Cavedale Road. He told us to go around to the next road across the valley to the south. Again we found a patrolman at that intersection with the highway and he wouldn't let us through. He treated us like sightseers. We told him we lived on Cavedale Road and that forestry wanted us to reoccupy our home. He was adamant. His orders were to keep everyone out of the Cavedale area. He talked through the open car window explaining. In the back seat, Tang stood up on the mesh of his cage and screamed directly into the officer's face.

To be consciously anthropomorphic, I felt that he said plainly enough: "You goddamed fool, I've got to piss." The officer drew back, shaking his head. Then he waved us through.

The cats were quiet now. I think they recognized where they were when we climbed the steep grade to the house. I pulled to a stop in the carport. We were surrounded by a grey and black stillness. We took the cats into the family room and opened the cage and the carrier. They had been confined for seven hours. All three headed for the flexport.

I wish I knew what went through their brains as they emerged into that strange world outside. Everything not burned to ashes was scorched until the tree leaves were dried brown like a sudden autumn. All around us smoldered a great silence. All bug clamor had ceased. Only the voice of a pumper truck radio at the house across the ravine indicated there was anything living besides us.

Tang and Charlie each had their special privy places and set out for these spots regardless of the desolation. But Topsy's toilet place was closer and we watched her come around to the front of the house. She seemed to tiptoe along, testing the ash and burn, looking about big-eyed, not as if she were afraid, but rather appalled by all she encountered. As Ruth said, "Like a little old lady, tsk, tsk, tsking" at this devastation of the world she had known.

While we were abroad a few years ago, a friend "house-sat," and "cat-sat" for us. It was late spring and Manville, the sitter, had to take Curley to the vet to have a "foxtail" removed from the edge of his eye. The red tabby didn't protest the carrier either going or coming. And he was patient and calm when the doctor removed the barbed seed. The experience didn't seem to bother him.

The next morning, Manville told us later, Curley sat on the rug in front of the fireplace and looked up at him; then, with what appeared to be an effort, he opened the eye that had been treated very wide as if to show how much improved it was. His behavior was predictable. Curley's only travels in a car were to the vet, and with the exception of the time he was neutered, they had all been to take care of an injury or something that resulted in his feeling better.

But Tang had different experiences. The weekend before we were to return, he refused to eat and by Monday a swelling appeared on his jaw. Manville called our vet for an appointment.

All the way to the vet Tang protested. He always did. The doctor found an abscessed tooth and insisted that Tang must stay overnight in the hospital. That was a situation I had always avoided with Tang, but Manville didn't know my reasons or what to do about it. Later, he told us that he had never seen such a look of being betrayed as the look Tang gave him when the cage door closed on him.

An exaggeration? Hard-core anthropomorphism? But just what did go through Tang's mind at the moment? Perhaps nothing? Just fear?

The next morning we came out from the San Francisco Airport on the bus and Manville picked us up at the bus station. We stopped at the clinic for Tang and took him home with us. He was happy we were back and glad to get home. Curley was there to greet him but Si had spooked when Manville took Tang away the previous morning and he hadn't been seen since.

After we unloaded our luggage Ruth called Si. No sign of him. Tang went around outdoors calling. It wasn't until after lunch that the young Siamese put in an appearance, coming up the drive. Tang went to meet him and they sniffed noses. When he came up to us there was no spookiness, or reticence, or shyness. We weren't strangers, though we'd been gone two months. The tip of his tail tapped his spine ecstatically. He seemed to rejoice: Tang was back, his real folks were back; all his world has come together again. At dinner Tang ate with enthusiasm; Si took his place behind his dish and gobbled his food; and Curley waited politely at the corner of the sink cabinet until Ruth issued his ration. That evening Si slept hard on Ruth's lap. Tang luxuriated on my lap. And for some strange reason, Curley who, in our absence, had appropriated Manville's lap, returned to his red chair, where he usually slept when we were home. Manville was left alone, a guest in the house, just a friend of the family. Us real cats were all together again.

We talked about our trip; Manville reported on the happenings in the neighborhood while we were away. In the morning, Tang, Si and Curley went with Manville to his VW Camper and "helped" him load up to leave. They liked him, but he was not part of their family.

7

What Is Your Cat to You: Pet or Friend?

When news is slow for the media—no hijackings, international incidents, murders, rapes, robberies—the non-human animal stories that have piled up on the spindle are pulled to entertain readers and listeners. Cats always get their share of this "filler" air time and newsprint space:

There was Sgt. Ralph, the unflappable crime fighter on the "rat patrol" of a police department. Shava was a cat that made her home in one of the University of California libraries until two students busted her because one was allergic to cats and the other was afraid of them. Then there's the person who is about to be evicted because of too many cats, or who has been evicted and is now living in a station wagon surrounded by these many cats.

Occasionally an unusual story comes to light like "The Cat Woman" who rescues cats from high places. She's sixty-one years old but a master at throwing a lanyard around a tree or pole and spiking her way to the stranded feline.

One of the most poignant of such stories to come to my attention is of a fireman who rescues a woman trapped by flames, then brings out her cat overcome by smoke. He tries mouth-to-mouth resucitation but his efforts fail. When someone asked him why he bothered to try, he replied, "It was a life."

That is the issue: *A life is worth saving!* A living being is worth saving, observing, understanding, knowing. Most people have been trapped into the idea that non-human lives are a waste of time. Why bother about saving a "pet"?

A reviewer of Muriel Beadle's fine book, *The Cat*, points out that she "scrupulously tried to avoid 'human' words" and that Judy Fireman in *Cat Catalog* said she "decided that if this one (book about cats) was going to be interesting, it would have to be scientific."

Without wishing to be critical, I'd like to point out that all words are "human," and being "scientific" has as broad a meaning as the whole human language, or as narrow as the jargon of one narrow scientific field. Both Ms. Beadle and Ms. Fireman wrote about cats under the unscientific influence of an ethic that says a mythical deity created Man, then a host of lesser animals, including the cat, with which Man is to amuse himself.

It seems to me unscientific to consider the functioning of the basic brain of Man separate from the functioning of the basic brain of any other animal. The only difference is in the respective "frames of reference." These are the experiences that conditioned the brain of the animal we are observing, whether it be human or non-human, man or cat.

To communicate these observations we have developed *human language.* Non-human animals have their own forms of communication.

We knew a young couple with a small mongrel dog named Charlie (the same name as our black-and-white cat but the two animals never knew each other). The dog Charlie rode on the young couple's motorbike when they came to visit us. He was clean, quiet and friendly, and made no aggressive gestures toward our cats. When winter arrived he came into the house with his people.

Our cats were Tang, Curley, Mao and Missy Manx. Only Missy Manx felt intruded upon and we had to watch to keep her from attacking the visiting dog.

One time Charlie sat on a corner of rug with one of his people close to the fireplace. Missy Manx came in through the flexport, ate from her dishes, then joined the rest of us in the family room. When she got to the corner of the rug diagonally opposite Charlie, she stopped. She glared at him, but neither hissed nor spat. I saw her raise one front paw, all claws out, and rake the empty air in front of her directly toward Charlie. The little dog neither barked nor growled. He just bared his teeth, chattered them together a little and wrinkled his nose. There was six feet of space between them.

It seemed to me that Missy Manx said very plainly, "I'll scratch your eyes out!" And Charlie replied, "I'll bite your leg off!" After this silent exchange they both settled down.

When I interpret the behavior of my cats I check their actions by what I believe to be their frames of reference against what my own brain's frames of reference tell me I might do in a similar situation. The basic pattern of action will be the same. Of course, I can be wrong. But "scientific" people make mistakes too.

All too often observations and interpretations of animal behavior are rejected because such do not fit the frames of reference blessed by a Jane Goodall or Dr. Conrad Lorenz. That is not to disparage either Ms. Goodall or Dr. Lorenz, but the "last word" on animal behavior has not been said, and probably never will be said.

Ms. Emily Hahn in an article for the *New Yorker* magazine quotes Charles L. Hanson, curator of birds and mammals, Arizona-Sonora Desert Museum in Tucson: "Why animals react as they sometimes do to strangers is a puzzle. I know there are criticisms of observations made in a zoo, on the grounds that the situation is so artifical that such observations have no validity. I don't think that's true. Even in an artifical situation, the animals still reflect intelligence levels, communication levels, and behavior patterns that are characteristic and valid, and these should be given serious consideration, because, after all, they simply cannot be made in the wild. It's the only opportunity we have to document. I think most poeple are beginning more to accept such knowledge. When we see the relation between bobcats and human beings here, for instance, there's no reason to suppose that it differs radically from communication between bobcat and bobcat in the wild. Certainly we shouldn't just ignore it, though the interpretation, of course, is always open to question. I must admit that here at the museum we are emotionally involved with our animals, and such involvement precludes objectivity. Even so, the observations themselves are valid. Interpretations by other people are quite all right as long as one doesn't throw out the material."

I agree completely. What he says goes for observations of animal behavior outside the zoo, domestic animals and in my case—cats.

A not uncommon belief about cats is that their only interest in humans is as providers of food, shelter, comfort and affection. As long as such is forthcoming any provider is acceptable. The cat doesn't propose to give anything in return.

In our family, Ruth usually provides the food and I provide the fire in the fireplace. Our cats thank us by rubbing against us, purring and butting their heads into whatever part of our anatomy is available. If Ruth doesn't feed them all they want, or what they want, or when they want it, they will come and tell me about it. (That statement could get me accused of thinking I know what goes on in a cat's mind "internally," and also of being the author of a "sentimental book" about cats. The question is: can a cat possibly recognize any other favor a human might do for it?

In the late 30s I worked for the Federal Writers Project in Albany, New York. I went up there from Cold Spring-on-Hudson Monday mornings and returned home Friday evenings. At that time we hadn't been cat-watchers seriously for more than a half dozen years. I suspect that we were still imbued with the idea: Me, human; cat, animal. At best, we considered them pets.

One Sunday night we had friends staying over and were up later than usual. I hadn't been asleep long before I was awakened by a cat crying on the roof. My first impulse was to try to get back to sleep and let him get down on his own. After all, he'd gotten up there, hadn't he? I wasn't successful. I knew that the only way I would get any sleep at all was to get that cat down. So I went out to see who was in trouble.

The flashlight beam revealed Leo IV, who weighed close to twenty pounds at the time perched on the roof ridge like a golden pumpkin. This was our second house in Putnam County and the pitch of the roof was so steep that a human couldn't walk on it. I was a premature A-framist, but the A-frame began ten feet from the ground on the front side. The rear of the structure backed into the slope of the hill and the eaves on that side came to about three feet from the ground, not a difficult jump up for a cat. The composition shingles gave Leo claw-hold going up, but not enough, because of the steep pitch, for coming down. I could appreciate his fear of trying. He was so fat that if he lost his hold he'd likely roll down and burst like an over-ripe melon.

My 20-foot ladder leaned against the roof didn't put me within reach of him. I tried to coax him down to me but he wouldn't budge. I got my six-foot stepladder, left it folded, and laid it on the roof, the lower step resting on the end of the longer ladder. This was a precarious arrangement, but I was still half asleep, in my pajamas and a fine drizzle had begun.

After climbing to the top of this ladder arrangement and lying flat against the roof, I could just reach Leo. I pulled him on to my shoulder and worked my way back down to the ground. I told him what I thought of his scene in not very friendly language, removed the two ladders and went back to bed. Five o'clock, and train-catching time came all too soon, and I was in no humor to speak to Leo that morning.

By the following Friday when I got home the whole incident had faded in my mind. I greeted Tersh, the older cat, and Leo as usual, and Ruth and I ate dinner. Afterwards, we took our respective places beneath the oil lamp and read.

Then Leo climbed into my lap, pushed aside whatever I was reading and began rubbing me with his jaws, butting his head against me and purring like a well-oiled motor. I had been going away and returning weekly for several months and he had never behaved like this before. It was Ruth's suggestion that his actions might be connected with my rescuing him from the roof in the rain. There was no way to prove that. He certainly wasn't showing me affection because I was the food provider or did anything else that pleased him.

All that weekend he followed me around like a shadow. fawning over me at every chance or just sitting and staring at me with a look that might have been interpreted as awe, adoration, or gratitude. He continued to treat me as something special for many weekends after. In time his attitude toward me put me back into the class of just an ordinary member of the family.

Give a cat the opportunity and he will find the most comfortable place in your home to sleep. Our cats have always found the base of an oil lamp something special to curl up around. For ten years we read by such a lamp in the evenings. It was one of those circular-wick models that gave a fair amount of illumination, also considerable heat.

At our cottage in the woods in New York State that lamp stood on a file box that sat on a trunk by the window at the end of the porch we had converted into a living room. The number one cat had the privilege of curling up around its base and sleeping there. If the number one cat wasn't home, the number two cat could assume the spot.

When we moved to the house with the steep roof up the hill, we still used oil lamps to read by for a year or more. Although the arrangement was somewhat different, there was still room for a cat around the lamp base. I'm sure our cats never felt that electricity was ever an improvement when we got it.

At the end of May that year, Tersh was drowned in an open well. When I retrieved the soaked body, I brought it up and let Leo see it. He sniffed it and turned away. There couldn't have been the slightest smell of his brother left. This body must have seemed to be but a cold, soggy object to Leo. We concluded that Leo didn't miss his brother. At the mention of Tersh's name he didn't show any sign of recognition. He acted as if he had no memory of him. Yet if he had recognized Tersh was dead, what could he have shown? He could not say to us, "Yes, I know he's gone." All he could have known was that his brother would not return. He was alone.

In our ignorance of cats at that time—they were still only pets to us—I don't believe we even considered that a cat might get lonely. After all, loneliness is a form of remembering. Some people even think cats have short memories. Besides, cats are supposed to be self-reliant, independent— the animal who walks alone, and Leo was very much alone now.

Two weeks after Tersh's death Ruth and I joined another couple for a trip through the Adirondacks checking tours for the New York State Guide. The middle-aged pair who bought our cottage in the woods promised to look after Leo, and feed him twice a day while we were gone. After all, that's sufficient consideration for a cat, an animal—food twice daily—isn't it?

When we returned we found his dishes full. We called him and after a while he came. He ignored us completely. He didn't respond to our greetings, petting, or our show of pleasure in seeing him. He treated us as if we didn't exist. Instead, he went straight to his dishes and began eating as if he were famished. After finishing off his food and tanking up on milk he went outdoors again, still ignoring us.

The woman who had looked after him said he hardly ate while we were gone. A little maybe, she could never be sure, but only a little at most. Every time she put fresh food in his dish he would sniff it and turn away. She tried various ways to coax him to eat. After dark he would come down to their house, which had been his home for five years, and cry, and call on the terrace steps. She'd go out and pet him and talk to him. She even tried to feed him there but he wouldn't eat. After a time he'd go away, probably back up to the new house, his new home.

Ruth had dinner to prepare and I had chores to do and Leo's reaction to our return got lost in activities. If anything, I think we felt a little hurt. When dusk came we lighted the oil lamp and took our usual places on either side of it to read.

Then Leo came. This time he welcomed us, climbing first into one lap, then the other, rubbing his jaw against us, butting us, purring. After his previous aloofness, this effusive demonstration seemed startling. Finally he ended his show of affection and curled up under the lamp. He went into a deep sleep, as if he hadn't slept for a week.

And maybe he hadn't slept, at least not much. He loved to sleep under that oil lamp of an evening. We realized that perhaps the absence of that lighted lamp for a week might have been what he missed the most. Now the lighted lamp and the two of us in our usual places completed the world he had known. His family, his food, his warm place to sleep of an evening must have been a very positive memory while we were away. After all, isn't what he missed a real basis for friendship, companionship in humans? So why not cats?

I think it was then I began to feel that my cats were more than pets to me.

It was that same Leo and his half-brother Timmy we brought to California. Leo never knew any of the Siamese who came to live with us, but Timmy did. He knew Tiki and Topsy. And that last summer, when it became obvious that he wouldn't be with us much longer, we were offered another Siamese. He was neutered and had all his shots—a year old, we were told, perhaps a little more.

This happened because my collaborator on "how-to-do-it"

articles and I dissolved our partnership and the shop-studio office-pool complex we had used in our how-to work had been sold to a young woman who planned to convert the place into a home. Now, another woman, in the process of separating from her husband, planned to move in with her. The Siamese cat belonged to this person, or to her husband. The two women brought him over one afternoon. He was a beautiful seal point. His name was Chiang.

Ruth and I and these women sat in the living room of our first house in California, talking, waiting to see how Chiang would react to his new home. After one look around, he came straight to me, climbed into my lap, put his paws on my shoulders and rubbed his jaw against mine. Why me? I don't know. Perhaps he was the husband's cat and that was why the woman was giving him away.

Anyhow, his show of affection got to me—we were friends. Then he went over to Ruth and gave her the same treatment. Not once did he pay any attention to the people who had brought him. When they prepared to leave and tried to say goodby to him, he ignored them completely. He smooched on Ruth's shoulder while I showed our visitors out, thanking them for the gift of the cat.

His behavior baffled me. He seemed to know that this was to be his home and wanted to win approval. At the same time he seemed aware that he had been given away, could do nothing about it and felt hurt. If he had been the husband's cat perhaps he missed the one person in his former family for whom he had developed affection. That could explain why he came to me—he was man-oriented.

In those formative months in a kitten's life, perhaps a good mother conditions it to go forth and find a new home and make a place for itself in the world. The people who accept it are its people, and the area around and about is its territory. But to be given away after being settled might indicate failure to a young cat. It could be a traumatic experience.

That sort of upheaval *is* for children. When catastrophe happens in a family and a child is passed on to new parents, a new family and new surroundings, no one would believe that such a violent change isn't difficult for a small kid to handle. But such a change can be explained to a child. It can't be explained to a cat. Or can it?

At the time Chiang came to us, our other cats were Timmy, the last of the red tabbies brought from New York, Topsy the Siamese spay, and Charles Addams, a black-and-white. We wondered what the bringing of a new cat into the home would involve, one not instructed in the rules of conduct of our home as a kitten. This had never happened to us before.

The first thing we did was to change his name to Tang. We couldn't abide the one he'd been given. But Tang sounded near enough like it so that we reasoned that he needn't be confused by the switch.

There were rough moments in his relationship with the other cats. He was afraid of Timmy. Apparently he'd never seen a red tabby before. Charlie and he kept out of each others' way. Topsy liked to sit on my lap after breakfast while I finished my coffee and had a cigarette. When Tang tried to get up on it she lashed out at him. But that was the only hostility she showed him. Maybe it was because he was Siamese that he won her acceptance so quickly.

That first night he didn't use the sandbox I made for him in the house. After breakfast I took him outside. He wouldn't use the dirt either. That day Anne removed the dirt from a flower bed to make way for new topsoil. In the evening I showed Tang this soft silt. All that powdery softness broke down his restraints. He dug a hole and used it. From then on he went outdoors to do his privy, but he never went back to that pile of silt and he never let me see where he did go.

His induction into our home seemed to be working out. But within a week a problem took shape. The shop-office studio-pool complex where the two women lived who gave Tang to us, was not more than 300 yards away on the drive, and closer, but not visible through the brush and trees. That had made no difference at first because Tang apparently didn't like those two women.

Then the woman whose marriage was breaking up brought a poodle over to live at the pool house. We heard it yapping. Tang heard it. It had been a friend of his, we were told, when he lived at his former home. The day after the poodle arrived, Tang disappeared. The two women worked during the day and weren't home. Ruth, looking for Tang, found him at the pool side, sitting with his poodle friend. He let her pick him up and bring him back to our place.

I felt that this was a serious situation. Tang wouldn't stay with us as long as his dog friend lived close by. Whenever he got lonely he'd go visit the poodle.

The next day he went over again. But this time he came home when Ruth called. That gave us a feeling of winning—he might just go visiting, then come home. However, the next time he went, he stayed and had to be brought back.

An afternoon later I happened to be out in our carport when he started down the drive. I followed. I knew where he was going and tried to talk him out of it. I didn't overtake him and pick him up, which I could have done, I just talked and explained and coaxed. Occasionally he would stop and look back. At the turn in the drive, I put everything I had in my attempt to win him. I felt that I had to persuade him to return, because catching him and restraining him was no solution. He just looked around at me, as if trying to assure me that he didn't want to be unfriendly but this was something he had to do. Then he walked on down the drive.

I went back to the house feeling helpless and defeated. We had lost him. We could never get him really to stay with us, I told Ruth, as long as the dog was over there.

Later Ruth decided to go after him once more. As usual the two women were at work. She found Tang and the poodle by the pool. Tang didn't object when she picked him up and carried him home. All the way back she explained over and over that he was our cat, we were his family now, that our home was his home and that we loved him. She put him down in the kitchen, knowing that all he had to do was go out the cat door and return to his friend. Unless we kept him shut in the house, it appeared there was no way to make him stay with us. We told ourselves we had done our best to make him understand.

As far as we knew, he never went back to visit the poodle. If he did, he always returned to his new home. Ruth and I have often wondered if it was her talking to him on the way back that last time that finally won him over.

Maybe her talk meant nothing to him; just words. Perhaps he was tired of walking over to that place, or perhaps he and the poodle didn't have anything to say to each other.

A few afternoons later I was in the shop side of the carport getting ready to work on a how-to project. Tang strolled in from the patio and stood looking down the drive. I joined him, wondering if he was going to take off again.

He looked up at me, our eyes met, and he leaped straight at my shoulder. I felt the tips of his claws tug the fabric of my shirt, and he settled himself around my neck like a live fur collar. That began eighteen years of the closest, truest friendship with any living being I have ever experienced.

At the end of six months, the woman who bought the shop-office-studio-pool complex lost her job and was forced to sell. She, her companion and the poodle moved away.

8

Are Felines Psychic? Or Are Humans Psychotic?

Perhaps the answer to both questions is, "Yes." When Extra Sensory Perception (ESP) and cats come under consideration we are dealing with one of the most exciting angles of cat-watching. Of course, it'll produce more skeptics than any other.

Many people refuse to believe in ESP. They can't accept its existence and anyone who does, and cites examples has, they believe, a very loose and questionable imagination. I keep an open mind, and I do find fun in observing my cats and fitting certain of their behavior into the parameters of ESP.

The feline afficionado Jean Burden has researched cat ESP. One instance she reports is a cat named Gypsy who always awakened his owner at the right time and shifted an hour ahead when daylight savings time came in and back when it went out. But his owner always had to tell Gypsy when the shift was made and which way. The owner felt that because the cat couldn't understand English or read clocks the communication between them had to be telepathic.

It's possible that Gypsy's owner had done a lot of talking to him in the "formative period" in cats, posed by the Harvard biologists, which in humans might enhance their word knowledge. And that could mean the cat really understood English. But no matter how you look at it, you have to admit that the cat's behavior was remarkable.

Ms. Burden's own cat could anticipate the arrival of her husband from work. Many cat owners can point to similar clairvoyance in their cats. But Honore Balzac had a cat who went to meet him when he came home from work. If he didn't plan to come home, she didn't bother to go out. And he didn't have to tell her in the morning that he wasn't coming home.

"Clairaudience" is another facet of ESP and Ms. Burden tells about a cat who hated the ringing of the telephone. It could anticipate an incoming call and knock the phone off the cradle before Ma Bell could ring. If one could train it to anticipate the nature of the incoming calls and only knock the instrument off for crank calls, maybe obscene calls, that would put the cat's talents to good use.

Stories about cats traveling long distances to return to their homes are common. Sometimes cats have followed their families to new homes thousands of miles away where they have never been. This is called psi trailing and cases have been investigated and substantiated by Dr. J. B. Rhine, former director of Duke Univesity's Parapsychology Laboratory.

Personally, I've never known cats to do anything spectacular in this ESP field. Friends had a cat that made trouble in their cat family. They gave him to some people they knew living more than ten miles away. He was back home in twenty-four hours.

Our daughter and family moved from one house to another several miles apart in Riverside, California. Her Siamese cat, Tom, found his way back to the other home in a couple of weeks. This was especially interesting because the home he had been taken to had been Tom's first home. He grew from kittenhood there. But the place he returned to had better hunting grounds nearby.

This poses a question: when a cat sets out for some place, does he *know* where he is going? Is there some "knowing" connected with his actions? It's like a cat seeing colors. Scientific minds still debate that subject but perhaps a cat "knows" a particular color.

Our Siamese especially show a preference for pillows covered with red corduroy to prop themselves against when they sleep. They reject cushions covered with aqua corduroy. I've been told that it's because the red is warmer. Yet give them a choice, hot day or cold, and they'll choose the red ones.

Si, a Siamese, was able to spot a skink which has an electric blue tail from twelve to fifteen feet away. It lay absolutely still, brown leaves camouflaging the rest of its body. If all Si had been able to see were shades of grey, as some people believe, he wouldn't have been able to spot that lizard at his cat's eye level. Movement? Ruth, who observed this, saw none. She could see that skink's electric blue tail distinctly among the leaves. Perhaps Si simply "knew" that lizard was there; that puts him in the "precognition" ESP category.

I was first aware of this "knowing" with our first Leo. A thunder storm blew up the day we finished moving from our original cottage in Putnam County, New York to one deep in the woods. Leo had been gone all day. We tried to let him know we had moved but he didn't come to whistling or calling. We decided that when the rain came and he went down to the old place he'd just have to make out the best he could. After the rain we'd try to find him and bring him over to our new place.

Thunder crashed; huge drops splashed. Ruth and I were in the living room of the new cottage. Just as the deluge started Leo leaped to the front window ledge, looking frantic. I opened the casement and let him in. He was home with his family.

How did he know enough to come over there? The houses were almost a quarter of a mile apart, our new one hidden in white birch and oak. Leo knew this new place—one of his patrol stops. And it was here, in this unfinished house the previous summer, that he and I first met. But how did he know we were there now? Maybe he heard us calling. Maybe he went to the other house, jumped to a window ledge, saw that it was empty of furniture, and came looking for a place with furniture he remembered.

Good reasoning? Yeah, but the other house wasn't empty. We had left part of our furniture in it for friends who planned to occupy it. The house still had some of the appearance of the home he knew. So he couldn't have come hunting a house with furniture he recognized. I felt that he was looking for us when he sat on that window ledge. He had an image in his brain that he wished, a little frantically perhaps, to match up with ourselves in reality. Or maybe he knew where we were all the time. He had just cut it a little fine getting there. Then again, maybe he'd only made a lucky guess.

I've often wondered about a cat's sense of "knowing." When my cats are outside, do they know where we are all the time, where the neighbors are, and the neighbors' animals? Perhaps they become disturbed when something strange moves onto the mental radar screen they have scanning the world around them.

Most of our cats have been spooky around strangers. Maybe they just like to give themselves a chance to evaluate newcomers from a distance, a postion of safety. Our second Leo, Sec, seemed more spooky about strangers than any of the others. His many encounters with danger and injuries could have conditioned him.

We didn't have many callers at this cottage deep in the woods—strangers, that is. It wasn't easy to find. Friends came out from New York City and our cats knew them and accepted them. It was Depression times and we didn't have friends with cars so most visitors came by train and I brought them out from the Cold-Spring-on-Hudson station in our Model-A pickup.

The cats were allowed the library table in the front room. In winter the sun shone through the door glass making a proper spot for a cat to sleep in. If a caller showed up, the cat or cats usually took off to some other part of the house. Approaching footsteps, not ours, were enough to trigger flight. If a cat still hesitated, it took only a knock to send him streaking.

One afternoon a knock brought me to see who had ventured this far back into the woods. I opened the door to an old friend who had been to visit us several times, but we hadn't seen him for at least six months. We had no telephone so he couldn't let us know he was coming. He had just hitch-hiked out from the station. We were glad to see him and our greetings were effusive.

After the welcome was over, I realized that Sec still sat on the table, within touching distance of any of us. His paws were folded under his chin as he calmly observed all that was going on, undisturbed by approaching footsteps, the knock or noisy greeting.

Why hadn't he fled at the sound of footsteps? Why hadn't he taken off at the first knock?

Sec knew Fred, our friend. Perhaps he liked him. If that was the answer it meant that his memory spanned a long period because he hadn't heard Fred's voice in a long time. And Fred had never arrived on foot and knocked. Previously I had brought him out from the station. Any stimuli for remembering couldn't have been strong because Fred had never stayed more than three days at a time.

Maybe that was enough. It's easy to forget that a cat's brain is not cluttered with the quantity of input besetting the human brain. Fred could have etched a clear frame of reference with all the details for recognition in Sec's brain.

It's easier to argue that just this once, Sec didn't feel like moving; he didn't feel like recognizing his conditioned reflex of flight. The answer might be that simple, but that denies basic mammalian reactions. Knowing Sec, I can't accept such an easy answer. However, I have no way to prove that Fred fitted into that red tabby's precognitive aura.

Until our cats had their own means of ingress and egress, they always seemed to know where we were in the house. In the daytime they came up the cat-ladder at the cottage. When we moved to the stone house up the hill they came to a door downstairs or jumped to a terrace table at a front window where they could be let in. At night they jumped to the bedroom window ledge in the cottage, and at the stone house, they used the cat-ladder to our bedroom. They always seemed to know where we worked, read or slept.

Perhaps "knowing" results from the cat's acute senses of smell and hearing which add up to a radar effect. Here in California I watched a friend's Siamese enter her living room, go to each of four guests present and sniff them, then go to the hearth and jump to a spot on the mantel where she liked to sleep. As the cat settled down for her nap, our hostess told us that she was blind. Her actions had been as sure as if she had sight.

The Leo we brought out here must have had a similar knowing sense developed after he became blind a few months before he died. One night when I came home from Chess Club Ruth told me that he'd gone out and hadn't returned. I took the flashlight and went looking for him. I called but he didn't answer. Was he somewhere lost, scared, blind, expecting me to rescue him and I was failing? Maudlin? Maybe. But to me a cat's brain must have the imprint of previous crises—for Leo the time I got him off the roof in the rain—and a new crisis would program the memory of a previous one and its solution. Or is a crisis, say a fear crisis, just a squiggle in the gray matter of a non-human brain, and nothing more? To me a stimulus activates a related imprint on the cortex and it's the same with a cat as with a human. I prefer to feel that I am being empathetic with my cats rather than anthropomorphic.

For more than an hour I searched, returning from time to time to see if he might have come home. When I was about to set out again, he came around the unfinished end of the utility room wall. His tail was up, his eyes wide but seeing nothing, or at the most only brightness, and he seemed happy to have found home, or happy that his "knowing sense" had returned him to his family.

Many years later this "knowing sense" was obvious in Tang in our second home here in California. Tang had the bad habit of catching and eating lizards. Apparently he preferred eating something he caught to canned cat food. Or maybe when he caught a lizard he felt that he had to follow through on a well-conditioned habit pattern of catch-and-eat even if it made him sick. Lizards are a bad diet for cats, and they are valuable little creatures to have around.

To discourage Tang, I took the lizard away from him when he caught one and turned it loose. Unless I went to a lot of trouble to hide it, he would recapture it. Sometimes he would let one loose in the house. I'd catch it, and while he sniffed where he'd last had it, I'd take it out through the kitchen and back door, through the carport and beyond the woodlot and let it go. Many times on my way back to the house, I'd meet Tang emerging from the flexport. He'd trot past me and over to the exact spot where I had freed the little reptile.

How could he zero in on that exact spot? He was in the house while I took it out and freed it. Was it scent that he followed? I doubt it. I've tagged along after him straight to the place where I let the lizard go. There he'd sniff around, and if the lizard didn't move to attract his attention, he wouldn't find it. So, if an acute sense of smell was his secret for finding where I'd taken the lizard, then his long range sense was better than his short range sense.

Recently I took a dead lizard away from Missy Manx. She had been playing with it among the flowers and grass that margin our little patch of patio lawn. She kept on looking for it while I, as surreptitiously as possible, took it into the shop and put it in a rubbish bag. After I returned to the patio, she stopped her search, and without hesitation, went unerringly to that rubbish bag. It was at least one hundred feet from where she'd been hunting and completely out of her sight. If a sense of smell had led her to the lizard in the bag, why had she kept on sniffing where she last had it until I returned to my chair?

Ruth has an hypothesis about this like something straight out of science fiction. She says cats have a built-in TV pickup or TV ESP. Their minds see what is happening or has happened in other minds around them. Or they can tune in on what has happened in other minds around them and play it back.

When Tang concluded that his lizard was no longer in the house, he tuned in on me and replayed in his mind just where I had taken it. All he had to do then was retrace my steps. But when he got beyond the woodlot, he had to hunt the lizard again becuuse in his mind he hadn't seen the lizard, he only saw where I had let it go. And Missy Manx had behaved in just the same way.

Ruth takes this idea even farther. She feels that humans can communicate with perceptive cats by making their minds blank, then inserting into this blankness mental pictures of what they want to get across to the cat. I have seen this work, but certainly not under circumstances that would convince a hard-core, scientifically-trained researcher. The trouble is: if the cat doesn't want to play this game, it can just tune you out.

However, my cat-watching has led me to believe that cats can tune in on each other through solid obstructions.

In our second home here in the Valley of the Moon my desk is at right angles to windows looking out on a deck. Ours is a split-level house and below the living room where my desk stands and the deck is an apartment. This puts me high enough so that when I pause in my work I can look out over the valley while ideas and words surface from my unconscious. The 10×34-foot deck along the window is a fine place for cats to sleep in the sun.

One morning when I took one of my refresher pauses, I noticed Charlie, the black-and-white cat, lying at the west end of the deck. He rolled suddenly to his feet and crept on short-legs toward the opposite end. From his eye-level he couldn't see anything but tree tops in the turn-around island fifty feet away or the vineyards on the ridge above the Hooker Creek Canyon.

My first conclusion was that a bird in the trees had caught his attention. I saw no feathered action. His interest seemed over the edge of the deck and down the drive. I got up and went to the end window for a better view of the slope. A hundred yards down the hill the road made a bend and disappeared. Coming around that curve was Tang. Charlie couldn't see him from his position at the end of the deck. However, when Tang came farther up the hill the black-and-white saw him. He noticeably relaxed and waited for the Siamese to join him on the deck.

How did Charlie know of Tang's approach before he came into sight? The Siamese hadn't announced his coming from that far away. His paws couldn't have made a sound on the armour-coated surface of the driveway. Coincidence? Perhaps. I don't know.

Another time I was sitting on the deck when Tang and Charlie set out on evening patrol. The black-and-white turned off the drive to the right and went into an area of manzanita, toyon and rocks. Tang continued past the pumphouse 100 feet, then disappeared behind it. On the pumphouse side of the drive, nearer the house, a ledge of rock obscured the ground beyond.

At first I idly registered the actions of the cats. Then I saw Charles come out of the brush just below the deck and cross the drive to the turn-around island. He stopped and looked toward the pumphouse. Then he continued up past the island along the near side of the bank and the rock ledge.

From the height of the deck I could see nothing that might interest him and I could see well beyond what he saw at his eye-level. Suddenly he began to hurry, past the island, across the end of the carport and up the bank. He was at least 150 feet from the pumphouse now. However, before he reached the top of the rock ledge I saw Tang coming in sight on the far side. I could see Tang several minutes before Charlie could. I watched them come together and sniff noses, then continue on their prowl.

How was it Charlie knew where to intercept Tang? Maybe it was accidental. That's an easy explanation. Perhaps they had a prearranged plan to meet. There's no way to prove that. Yet, should that possibility be ignored? Or, there's a chance that they were mentally in touch with each other all the time.

Possibly Tang didn't fear being given away because that had happened to him once, after he was a mature cat settled in a home. Yet, I feel that we upset him a lot one time, and he could have been spared the stress had a few humans tried to touch his mind even from a distance.

When Mabel was our tenant Ruth and I took a trip to Mexico for a month. She offered to look after the cats, build a fire in our fireplace occasionally and watch TV in our family room to make them feel almost as if we were home.

There was one small catch: it was December and Mabel wanted to be away for three days at Christmas visting her family over in the Sacramento Valley. It didn't seem insurmountable. A teenage neighbor would look after the cats while she was away. Both Tang and Charlie, our two cats at the time, knew this kid. He was responsible and liked cats.

But we didn't consider Tang and his trauma—Tang the worrier.

When Mabel got back from her three-day visit, Tang was there to meet her. Nothing unusual about that. He stuck to her like a bur. He insisted on sleeping with her that night. This wasn't unusual either. She'd spoiled him by letting him sleep with her at other times.

Later she told us he went to sleep with his head on her arm and slept that way until her arm tired. She moved him over to the other arm. He went right on sleeping, almost as if he were in a stupor, until morning. She eased her arm from under his head and he continued to sleep until evening. Then he got up and went upstairs with her to be fed along with the black-and-white. She said he ate as if he hadn't eaten the entire time she was away—this was picky Tang who seldom ate very much at one time.

Mabel realized then that he hadn't slept while she was away and he hadn't eaten earlier. He had just waited. Waited for what? Did he in this apparent abandonment wonder what had happened to his world, to his people?

Like so many people who love animals, but never really observe them closely, Mabel hadn't considered the possible depth of Tang's feelings. It was the old "they're-only-animals" syndrome. "I'd never have gone," she said, "if I'd thought he'd take it the way he did." It's easy to shrug this off as unscientific and sentimental.

But how might the situation have looked to Tang? His family is away for longer than usual. Maybe time means nothing to a cat. I find that hard to believe, but no matter. We had provided him with a substitute family in the same house in the form of Mabel. She fed him upstairs in his usual place, built a fire in the fireplace for him, let him sit on her lap.

He had privileges in her apartment he didn't have with us when we were home. So he went along with our absence. We had been away before, many times, if not for so long. Then his surrogate family loads bags into her car.

Mabel had parked in front of the apartment while she prepared for her trip. She left the car doors open. She often parked in front of the apartment and left the car doors open, so this was nothing new to our cats. Yet, this time, Mabel told us, both Tang and Charlie climbed in and checked over her preparations.

Now what must have gone through Tang's mind? Nothing? They both knew this getting-ready-for-a-trip routine. When bags are loaded into a car, humans take off.

It's hard for me to believe that any serious observer could conclude that the only mental processes for those cats were smells, shapes and sounds. Other things must gather together in a brain, even a cat's brain, for that brain to function.

All this really disturbed Tang. Maybe it occurred to him

that we had been gone longer than usual. Weren't we coming back? After all, within his frame of references, Topsy, his favorite Siamese companion, had gone away, and as far as he knew, she hadn't returned.

Then Mabel packs up and leaves. The vibes of his brain reached out and out—emptiness. He waited all night on the step and Mabel didn't come. A teenager puts food out for him in the morning. He knows the kid but increasing worry kills any appetite he might have had. Charlie, timid about all people who are not his own family, only puts in an appearance after the boy is gone. No consolation came from his black-and-white friend.

Sure, I'm reading Tang's feelings through my own frames of reference. But how far different could his have been? I've seen his worried look at times. It was the same look I've seen in the eyes of a child. We can find out what's bothering a child. It can communicate in a burst of tears or in hesitant, frightened words. Maybe Tang had tried to communicate from the beginning; when the first bag came off the shelf, or the first hanger of clothes went onto the hooks in Mabel's car; but nobody paid any attention.

You might ask, "Why didn't Charlie get upset by Mabel's going away like Tang did?"

Maybe he did. He was never as demonstrative as the Siamese. Besides, why should all cats behave alike any more than people? And remember, Charles came to us as a kitten. He had stayed all his life with us. Hurts and scares had happened. He had changed houses; we had gone away and returned; other humans had fed him. He had never experienced a complete family dissolution after becoming a part of a family, and Tang had. Charlie could only have sniffed Tang's nose, "They'll be back." But even to Charlie, another cat, Topsy, hadn't come back.

I persist in reading human feelings into a cat's behavior. That interpretation can only be rejected by the narrow scientific approach which holds that it is invalid because it can't be repeated under laboratory conditions. Or on the equally narrow human approach which holds that a cat is a lower animal; any being that isn't human we can treat with small concern.

Ruth and I returned to our daughter's place in Riverside three or four days after this had happened to Tang. I telephoned Mabel to ask how everything was. She mentioned briefly how upset Tang had been by her going away. I told her the day we expected to be home but not the time because I couldn't be sure when we would get there.

Later that day Mabel told us that right after lunch, when Tang was asleep on her bed, she said to him, "Tang, your folks are coming home this afternoon." He didn't seem to hear her, she said.

Two hours later, he woke up, asked to be let upstairs to our part of the house. Within half an hour we arrived and he was at the door to greet us. When we were still fifty miles away Ruth started thinking, "Tang, we're coming. Tang, we'll be home soon." The thoughts repeated in her mind. She formed a picture of us arriving.

It's easy to argue that to infer that Tang picked up Ruth's thoughts is pure hind-sighting. But was it? As the curator of the Tucson museum said, "You can disagree with and reject the interpretations. But that doesn't invalidate the observations."

Another instance of rapport between Ruth and the cats occurred when I was researching and organizing the material for *Do Cats Think?* I read all the books I could find about cats. When they were in the house, Ruth read some of them. She always rose before me. She fed the cats, then stretched out on the couch to read.

One morning when she was reading *The House Guest* by John D. MacDonald, she became aware that Charlie and Tang were side-by-side on the rug staring at her. Those two, once rivals, once enemies, sometimes friends and companions, lay on their bellies, close together, paws folded and both were purring. Charlie's purr rumbled loud and clear, while Tang purred in his own soft way. They weren't hungry and teasing to be fed. They weren't even thinking about her lap (Charlie wasn't a lap cat anyhow.) At that moment Ruth felt that they were, in some way, perhaps by some contact with her mind, enjoying what she read as much as she was enjoying it.

Even a sharper happening occurred recently while I was working on this book. Our new Burmese, Benji, is so dark that when he sleeps in a shadow on the rug he becomes almost invisible. We got a white flea collar for him to help us locate him.

One afternoon I let him out the back door wearing his collar. Half an hour later he came in without it. I looked around outside but found nothing and for the next few days we didn't find it. One afternoon when Ruth went out for her walk which included any cat who wanted to go, she had said to Mao. "Mao, go find Benji's collar."

When she came in later, she said to me, "Mao says Benji's collar is on the roof."

I laughed. That was too farfetched for me. We do talk like that with our cats, and report that they reply such and so, but mostly it's just for our amusement. She insisted that Mao had gone up on the roof and played with something there. All of our cats go up on the roof, and there are hundreds of acorns there for them to play with. Benji might have gone up on the roof, but I couldn't see how he could have lost his collar up there. I didn't pay any further attention to Mao's tip.

Six weeks later, after the big rains started, I got up on the roof to check it and there was Benji's collar. When I brought it down, I didn't tell Ruth I'd found it. I said, "Didn't you tell me Mao said that Benji's collar was on the roof."

"I certainly did," she said. "Several weeks ago."

I showed it to her then. Personally, I can't boast of any contact with what goes on in the minds of the cats we've lived with. But I'm not sure they aren't able to tune in on the workings of my mind.

It was a number of years ago and our cats were Topsy, Tang and Charlie. Ruth had been visiting Anne in Riverside. During the six weeks she was away I took the cats for their daily walks. At no time did all three go together until the last evening before I was to make the 500 mile trip to bring Ruth home.

Why did all go this once? Why did they all behave amicably? Prospects of that long drive have always given me moments of apprehension. It's a dull trip to make alone. It's a hazardous trip. But that evening, before this long drive, to have my three cats around me and friendly with me and each other seemed like a good omen.

9

We Gave an Abandoned Cat a Home

At the age of three I had an orange tabby kitten. I called it "Butter." It was a barn kitten, not litterbox trained. It wasn't given a litterbox. It made a "mess" and was thrown out.

When I was eight years old we had a female Maltese farm cat, nameless, wild, "slinky" and thin. She received little care from the family. Oh, my brothers splashed milk for her in the upturned lid of a milk can when the cows were milked. She survived the Iowa winter by staying in the cowbarn, absorbing the body heat from the cows and burying herself in the winter supply of hay.

I remember seeing her skittishly waiting for her pan of milk, not letting anyone touch her, slipping away the moment she had licked up the last drop. That spring she produced a litter of four kittens—black-and-white, grey-and-white and a calico, maybe a tabby. By June the kittens, perhaps ten weeks old, came out of the barn looking for a share of the milk my brothers poured for the mother. I was cautioned not to try to catch them or the mother would take them away. Perhaps that was one of those myths about country-born cats.

Although we made no overtures to the kittens they didn't seem afraid of us. I remember rainy afternoons lying on the last of the winter's supply of hay and watching those kittens play. They stalked each other, pounced, tangled, tumbled, wrestled; they ambushed each other, had battles, free-for-alls, got into serious fights, then got over their seriousness. Their gyrations entertained my brother and me for hours.

The barn was again filled with hay. The kittens left the shelter of the haymow and joined us at milking time in the milk-yard. They continued their games and we watched while we milked. As autumn approach they disappeared. We wondered what had happened to them. A month later they showed up, were around for a few days, then disappeared for good.

The smoke-grey mother appeared at milking time, still a "fraidy-cat." We didn't mistreat her but made no attempt to be friendly with her. Her kittens were gone.

A year later my brother announced that he had seen the kittens at a neighbor's farm three-quarters of a mile away. Why they left us has always been a mystery to me. The old cat had more litters. Some stayed; some left. Their play never seemed to reach the crescendo of activity of that first litter.

It was at least thiry-five years before Ruth and I took in a stray cat. All our New York State cats were given to us as kittens, and we knew their parentage and background. There were the usual roaming tomcats during the oestrous period, but winters are bitter there, as bitter as in Iowa, and cats and kittens don't survive without some dependable source of food and shelter.

At lunch time one day in August, I heard our cats making threatening yowls outside. I went to investigate and found both Tersh and Leo IV squared off at a strange cat, a well-marked grey-and-black tabby tomcat. He didn't fit the usual type of roaming male. He didn't appear sick; he showed no hostility and no indication that he would defend himself if attacked.

I put our two red tabbies in the house and returned to find out what was wrong with him. He wasn't afraid of me. But he cried as if he might be hurting or hungry. I petted him and felt him over for injuries. He rubbed against me.

At that time I didn't believe in feeding stray cats. Anyone might be somebody's pet, and I didn't want to lure an animal away from its own people. (I've come to question that idea. The cat may be lost and hungry, and if fed could reorient itself and return home.) I didn't recognize this cat. He looked like a tabby named Teddy belonging to our nearest neighbor. I knew Teddy and he knew me, and more to the point, he knew our cats and never ventured into their territory. I talked to him, petted him, but offered no food.

I went back to my lunch, hoping he would go away, but he stayed around the house. That afternoon when I went over to the garden he followed me. I began shucking out the nubbins still on our first sweet corn stalks, tossing them to the path to be picked up later and given to our chickens. These were Depression times and we couldn't afford to waste anything. Some of the kernels were still soft with milk.

At first I thought this stray tabby was playing with the nubbins as I tossed them and they rolled in the path. Then I realized that he would hold one between his front paws and gnaw at the soft kernels. He was hungry, so hungry that he was eating raw sweet corn on the cob. Hunger is a condition that gets to me fast. I brought a bowl of bread and milk (standard cat food in the '30s) over to him. He ate all of it, then washed himself thoroughly.

I carried him over to the house, put him beside me on the seat of the pickup truck and started out to visit the neighborhood to see if anyone knew or wanted him. An old lady, half a mile up the Albany Post Road, recognized him. She told me that she thought he was dead. Her middle-aged, drunken son had hit him on the head with a stick and he had disappeared. He must have wandered in a half-conscious daze to our place.

She seemed genuinely glad to have him back. When I drove past a few weeks later I saw him on her porch. He never came back to visit us. I haven't been able to get the picture out of my mind of that tabby eating sweet corn nubbins, even though I've learned that some cats really like sweet corn.

During our sixteen years in Putnam County that was the only stray that came to us. Out here in California the climate is milder and humans dump their unwanted kittens in the country. The kitten population increases with the growth of the human population.

The red tabbies we brought from New York were still with us when a red tabby kitten showed up about ten o'clock one night. It may have been abandoned. But there were native red tabbies in the neighborhood and it may have simply been looking for its own home. A primordial urge had sent it forth into the world. Maybe its mother had just driven it off.

Timmy making threatening yowls in the carport brought me out to see what was going on. He had squared-off at this kitten beneath the Studebaker. The stranger might have been three or four months old. Timmy seemed quite definite about not wanting this feline sticking around.

If I had made up to the youngster Timmy might have accepted it. I wasn't in the humor at the moment. I might have reasoned, "He could belong to someone. He may have his own home. If I don't make overtures to him, he'll return to it."

I kept Timmy from attacking the kitten, and it went up the bank above the carport, picking its way with certain resolution as if it knew quite well what it was doing. I followed it with the beam of the flashlight for three or four yards.

It stopped and looked back at me with neither an expression of fear nor appeal, but rather, as I interpreted it: "I'd like to stay with you here, but that other cat doesn't want me. Unless you're willing to intervene, I'll just move on." And the red tabby kitten disappeared in the brush up the ridge. The look on its face is still with me after many years.

Not until a new development road was put up behind our property did we find what I was certain was a really "dumped" kitten. One November evening around Thanksgiving time a little grey cat with a white front showed up in the carport of our second house here in the Valley of the Moon. Ruth discovered it first. None of our cats seemed hostile toward it. I put out some dry pet food for it and it ate ravenously, mewing between bites and purring loudly. It danced around, tail straight up, but any movement toward it sent it scurrying to safety beneath the nearest car.

It was obviously a ranch cat and not accustomed to being handled. We felt certain it was female. What were we going to do with her? We had four cats at the time and it was out of the question for us to take another.

If we had the time and patience, we might be able to tame her and make an acceptable house cat of her. No matter how optimistic we were that would be a doubtful project. If we did domesticate her we might not find her a home. In the meantime, we might become attached to her, and it would be difficult to give her up. And five cats!

Suppose we were unsuccessful in taming her. We could always take her to the pound, but there they die a horrible death in a decompression chamber or are sold to a laboratory for experimentation.

I couldn't consider such an end for this wild little creature that had found her way to our door but something had to be done. I held disdain for whoever did this to this kitten and to me. I was trapped by my own feeling; forced to handle a distasteful job that I was in no way responsible for.

The following day I called our vet, told him the situation and asked if he would put her to sleep. He assured me he would. "It's the only thing to do," he said. "She hasn't a chance."

That didn't ease my miserable feelings as I caught the little grey-and-white mite, put her in a carrier and took her down to the clinic. The vet gently put her to sleep. I brought the little body home and buried it.

I didn't feel the spirit of Thanksgiving that year.

The lives of all dumped kittens do not end so tragically. A couple of months later, a lady living on our private road but closer to Cavedale Road, brought us a "rumpy" Manx. This little tom, not more than eight-weeks old, had been dumped in the canyon. Abandoned strays usually reached this woman first because she was nearer the county road and she found homes for them. This time she had to go to Sacramento the next day and couldn't handle this little fellow.

He needed care and Ruth cleaned him up. Whatever he had lived on between the time he was dumped and found our neighbor's place was no food for a kitten. We got some worm medicine down him and he vomited a load of brown, squirming parasites.

He was friendly and feisty—white with orange patches and no tail at all. Our older cats accepted him at once. By Monday morning he was eating normally, using a litterbox, and giving our cats a workout, taking on all comers. Again, with four cats, we couldn't take in another no matter how attractive he was.

I called the classified ad department of the local paper. It has a "come and get it" section: no charge for an ad if you want to give something away. I sent in an ad for little Rumpy.

The paper didn't come out until Thursday morning and I was afraid that by then we might become so attached to this friendly, feisty little character, that it would be hard to give him up. Suppose no one wanted him. But if a person went to the office the evening before, he could get a copy. We hadn't finished dinner that Wednesday when a call came inquiring about the little Manx. A young couple came out, saw the little orange and white Rumpy, loved him at first sight, and took him with them. They had two cats but one of them had just died.

We received nine other calls for that little character before the week was over. Several months later Ruth visited this young couple, and found little Rumpy, much much grown, sleeping blissfully, curled upon—naturally—a blue satin pillow. The story of all stray kittens should have such a happy ending.

Many roaming tomcats visit us, shopping for females in heat. Seldom do any show any signs of staying after a few encounters with the resident felines.

Like our cats, Ruth and I have special places where we sit. At one time in our present home, hers was on the couch with her back to the floor-to-ceiling windows in the family room; mine in the corner between fireplace and windows. From my spot I could see into the kitchen, and over my shoulder; I could look out at a flower bed between the window and the top of huge lava boulders on the edge of our ridge and beyond to all of the valley.

This particular morning I had brought up the mail. Ruth and I, seated in our usual places, were going through the daily collection. For some reason I glanced over my shoulder and there on one of those lava rocks, with its bright green skin of lichen, sat a red tabby staring at me. Perhaps his intense stare had prompted me to look around—some people think cats can do that. He was somewhat darker than our red tabby Leo line begun forty years earlier in New York State. But he had the same large head, wide-set eyes, stocky body. He didn't move when we made hard-eye contact and he wasn't more than three or four yards away.

I gave a surprised, "Hi, there."

Ruth looked around and saw him. We saw him open his mouth but no sound came out which reminded us of the "silent" miaow of our first Leo.

He didn't seem afraid. Rather, he seemed to be questioning, "Don't we know each other?" Then he walked close past the window and disappeared down among the lava boulders and live oak trees.

A look of rugged assurance about him impressed us. He

didn't seem hungry. We guessed that he wasn't a young cat; one ear appeared battle-chewed. He must live fairly close, perhaps on Moon Mountain Road, half a mile as the crow flies, or maybe even down on the highway. That thought brought with it the danger of traffic. We hoped his home was Moon Mountain. Spring had begun here in California, the time for toms to roam; perhaps he was just passing through.

A week later we saw him again on the rocks. He gave us his silent miaow greeting and went on his way. Then he appeared one night in our carport. He still seemed in good condition as if he had a home. He was shy but not unfriendly.

Our cats at the time were two Siamese: Tang, who had been with us twelve years, and Sci-Fi, not yet a year old. The red tabby showed no hostility toward them. Tang seemed to ignore him. Si avoided him, perhaps because he was twice the size of the young Siamese.

I talked to him and told him to go on home. He drifted off—I assumed because I offered no food and he had no excuse for staying around. Then he began putting in an appearance twice a week. We heard him at night going around the house calling. That convinced us that he was really just a roaming tom. On such occasions he had quite a normal tomcat voice. We always referred to him as the cat with the crinkled ear.

As he grew more friendly, a closer examination made me realize that although it resembled a wrestler's cauliflower ear, there is no way a cat can get such an injury. It had to be a birth defect—a "simple" ear was the term a nurse friend gave it, caused by resting too long in one position in the womb. A neighbor saw him, facetiously suggested that he'd caught "peach-leaf" curl, and that gave him his name: "Curley."

The season of roaming tomcats passed but Curley appeared more often and stayed longer. On his frequent visits he must have watched the Siamese negotiate the flexport, but he didn't make any attempt to come into the house. A tone of appeal gave more strength to his almost voiceless miaow but I'd tell him to go home. He'd be gone for a day or so, then show up again.

Ruth, an early riser, often found him in the carport or shop. She began to have the feeling that he wasn't as old as his *simple ear* made him look. Besides he seemed to be getting thinner. We speculated that, like many cats out here in warm weather, he was eating lizards which made him thin. His continued quiet appeal touched Ruth. She offered him a handful of dry cat food by the patio gate. He ate it hungrily.

After that first handout he disappeared but was back in a few days. Now we began wondering: did he really have a home? We gave him food in the carport, adding a dish of milk. He remained conspicuously polite to the Siamese though he outweighted both of them. Once Ruth brought him into the house to show some friends. As soon as she put him down, he dashed for the door and wanted out.

We began inquiring to see if anyone knew him. No one seemed to have seen this red tabby with a deformed ear. At last we stopped at a place on the highway, half a mile across the fields from our house. A very heavy woman told us he had been left behind by the family preceding her. "You can have him," she said.

One of Curley's traits that impressed us was his apparent respect for Tang and Si. He seemed to want very badly to play with them but they wouldn't play. They "snooted" him. We have always felt that Siamese cats have a racist streak.

Of course, Curley's size and *simple ear* bothered them. Even before we decided to take him in we noticed the trouble he had with that ear. We suspected ear mites but his size made us hesitate to help him. As summer heat and dryness increased his trouble seemed aggravated. He showed amazing dexterity when he tried to take care of it himself. Lying on his right side, he held the ear with both front paws, while he tried to clean it out with his left hind foot. Finally we decided to help him. He made little protest. Actually he seemed appreciative as I held him and Ruth cleaned out his ears with a cotton swab. He made no more protest than a sort of reflexive thumping of a hind leg on the table top.

He liked to be picked up and petted, purring his appreciation. If Tang were around, he'd struggle to get down as if he didn't want to make the old Siamese jealous. He continued to indicate his desire to fraternize with the Siamese but he never got farther than a friendly "murrp." Neither Tang nor Si showed any sign of being afraid of him, despite his size, but they made no overtures in his direction.

We soon discovered that Curley was fond of chicken, raw or cooked. So was Tang. Curley never tried to muscle in on the Siamese's share. At this time we noticed that Curley disappeared on weekends. We worried about him going across the highway to his former home. However, there were culverts for passage to the far side to avoid traffic.

After he had been gone a day or so, he'd suddenly show up. There he would be, curled up by the back step in the shade as if he'd been there all the time. Or as if he had just materialized to be near his new family. The next weekend he would be gone again.

Ruth's theory was that a family had befriended him after he was abandoned, and they always had chicken on Sundays. So he went back regularly for scraps. That notion was good for a laugh.

That fall I took him to our vet to be neutered and checked over generally. He had a bad case of ear mites in spite of our attempts to clean his ears. The doctor treated the problem. "Bang-ear," he called him. When I mentioned an *enteritis* shot, he said, "It'd be a waste of money. There's no way of knowing how old he is, but he's obviously built up an immunity of his own and doesn't need a shot."

Curley had to stay over night at the pet clinic. The next day I had to go into the city and the job of bringing him home fell to Ruth. If I take one of my cats to a place where he is going to suffer hurt, I want to be the one who rescues him from that place but this time was an exception.

However, Curley never seemed to blame me for what happened to him at the clinic. On the way there he had protested a little. Ruth said he didn't protest on the way home as soon as she told him where he was going. He recovered from his operation quickly.

Now Curley was a full-fledged member of our family, the first stray or abandoned cat we had ever adopted. This red tabby seemed almost a link to the six red tabbies we had in New York State.

That year, after the rains started, I got up on the roof to remove the spark screen from the chimney. To my surprise Curley came right up the ladder after me. Our New York red tabbies always liked to climb ladders. Leo IV and Timmy climbed ladders whenever they had a chance out here. I always assumed that they climbed ladders, people-ladders, because they used cat-ladders to get into their homes both in Putnam County and out here. None of our other cats, Siamese or non-Siamese, climbed people-ladders although they all used cat-ladders to get into our house. It seemed to be exclusively a red tabby trait. No matter when I put my ladder to the roof, if Curley is around, he will come gallumping up those rungs like a trained seal. It isn't possible, but he almost behaves as if he were a descendent of our original red tabbies, surfacing out here, after a gap of many years.

10

Romance and the Neutered Cat

An unneutered feline romance can be as touching and revealing as any people romance. After reading *Do Cats Think?* Margaret McDonald of Victoria, British Columbia, wrote me about her two cats, "a female Siamese named Katie and a male Persian named Robin. Robin and Katie mated and in due time Katie produced four kittens, two pure white, as is Robin and two a mottled black and brown. Like you we had heard stories of tomcats attacking kittens, so we were constantly on the watch during the first few days after birth. On the second day Katie got out of the box of sleeping kittens and, standing a few feet away, she let out a typical Siamese yowl. This woke the kittens, who started mewing. Robin heard the crying and came running into the room. Katie stopped her yowls, looked at the kittens then moved a few feet further away and sat down. She again looked back at the box, then moved again until she had reached the door of the room. Robin meanwhile looked back and forth between kittens and Katie. Finally he appeared to understand the message and moving over to the box he climbed carefully in and started licking the crying kittens. At last all was quiet as the kittens settled down to suck on Robin's long hair; only then did Katie leave to go outside. This performance was repeated each time Katie wished to leave the kittens and even when the kittens were eight-weeks old Robin continued his babysitting activities by assisting Katie in carrying her brood outside for hunting sessions. At no time did Robin discriminate between those two kittens that looked like himself and those two that didn't.

"A year later Katie produced another litter but Robin was not the father. She called on him a number of times in the first few days to babysit but he never responded. When the kittens grew to the playful stage he found them annoying and would bat them away if they attempted to attack his tail, something he had allowed the other kittens to do repeatedly. We could only assume from Robin's actions, that in some way he was aware that he had not sired the second litter of kittens. We had Katie spayed and Robin neutered after this, due to the problem of finding good homes for the kittens, so we were unable to see if another set of kittens fathered by Robin would get the same patient, loving attention from him as the first litter had, but like you we are cat watchers not scientific experimenters."

Neutering does not eliminate romance, only reproduction. Males are relieved of the drive to roam and fight—the chance of injury, mutilation and death; and females are no longer forced to produce unwanted kittens. If the male is neutered between six and ten months his sexual conditioning is not so firmly fixed that his relationship with other cats is influenced by it. What remains is companionship, mutual grooming, mutual protection and games. Individually, an adult cat's "padding" or "kneading" is a kind of sexual release. With neutered males it can result in minimal masturbation.

Kittens at play learn to hunt, fight and the pattern of the sexual game. The young tom pounces upon another cat, male or female, lands on its back, and bites its neck. This is a hunting routine if what he pounces on is a rabbit, rat, or squirrel. It is also just a game with one of his siblings. Unneutered, a time comes when internal pressures of hormones urge him to visit other cats. The strange oestrous scent of a female attracts him. Perhaps to his surprise, a female in season turns out to be easier to pounce. The pattern of his conditioning fits in with hers and they mate. Whoopie!

When the tom is neutered later than ten months the conditioned sex behavioral pattern is more rigid. The "fixed" male still follows pursuit and pounce habit patterns. Spayed females soon learn that the over-ten neuter plays this way. They don't like it. They distrust him. And a really friendly relationship can't exist between cats neutered late in life.

In February of the year Curley put in an appearance at our place, Si reached his eighth month and we had him neutered. The vet used one of the hallucinogenic drugs as an anesthetic and Si had a bad "trip" coming out of it. He wandered about disoriented for hours and we had to keep careful watch on him so he wouldn't get lost. It was several days before he was his old self. Shortly after his recovery the unspayed female of the family at the top of the ravine to the east of us came in heat and visited our cats. This family believed that only female cats are good hunters, and then only when they have kittens. Si's body still produced hormones but he was too inexperienced to know what to do.

So this little calico made a play for Tang. She would lie down and roll in front of him, put her front legs up around his neck and try all sorts of ways to get the proper response from him. He seemed to enjoy the attention, but he had been neutered a long time and could do nothing to satisfy her.

Curley was undoubtedly a roaming tom at the time, and he might have done something about the situation. We don't know. Perhaps it had been his visits to this calico that started him coming to see us. Anyhow, the neighbor's cat became pregnant, had her kittens and I suppose did her hunting to make up for the food she didn't get.

Meanwhile Curley started the long process of becoming our cat which led to his being neutered in the fall. As his hormone production dropped he wanted more than ever to play with Tang and Si but they continued to be stand-offish. Perhaps it was because they were Siamese royalty, or it could have been his deformed ear. Whenever they got a chance they sniffed that ear as if trying to figure it out. Then perhaps they felt there was too much tomcat still in him and they didn't want him to pounce on their backs and bite their necks.

The following spring the neighbor's calico came in heat again and visited us. Si was only curious about her. I talked to her and Tang was present. Last year he had been friendly to her, but this year, whether in a fit of jealousy because I paid attention to her or for some other reason, he attacked her and drove her away. Curley was away hunting at the time.

That afternoon, after our usual naps, we went outdoors with plans to do some yard work. Curley stood on the bank on the far side of the driveway. When he saw Ruth start over to the island flower bed in the center of the car turn-around, he came to meet her, walking high on his toes, talking loudly for a "silent miaow" cat, making what I interpreted as happy, coaxing sounds.

Ruth spoke to him and he hurried back over the bank. There was the calico cat. He rubbed against her, still talking in a high, insistent tone. He came back to Ruth and arched and rubbed against her. Back and forth between the two he trotted several times making beautiful trilling sounds.

We don't know what he was saying but it had all the signs of happiness and excitement, "Look, folks, I've found a friend. Isn't she beautiful? Isn't she wonderful? And she likes me."

The calico drifted off into the ravine to the east and Curley went along. Knowing that the neighbor expected his cats to forage for their food, Ruth suggested that Curley had been saying, "Please folks, let her stay here. We've got lots to eat. And I would have a friend, an American cat friend to play with."

She'd have stayed too, had we offered her food, but that wasn't what she wanted at the moment. The mechanics of her body had structured her behavior. We had deprived Curley of the ability to give her what her body demanded.

When her season passed or she found an unneutered tom, she returned to her home and foraging for food, and producing more unwanted kittens in the fifty-five plus days prescribed by nature. Curley returned to his home and his games. For that brief time he had behaved the way a happy child behaves, and I think he had been expressing the same emotions a happy youngster expresses.

Curley's games were of his own making, like galloping up and down the length of our roof. It made a sound like an approaching earthquake. In the house he loved to bunch up all the throw rugs in the place, then look around, quite pleased with his accomplishment. The Siamese still shunned him, partly because he never separated play from sexual aggressiveness not even after he was neutered.

In early August I found the desiccated remains of the calico cat that had been Curley's friend. She was in the ravine to the east. I asked the neighbor about it. All he knew was that she had disappeared.

Shortly after that, when I started out through the carport to the shop, I was startled by a demanding cry behind me. Between our car and our tenant's car sat a strange cat. It seemed wary, "Are you friendly?" It looked young and was perhaps a female. I spoke to it and it approached me, crying insistently, obviously hungry. I didn't recognize it as a neighborhood cat.

After determining that it was a female and not in heat, I brought her some dry cat food and a saucer of milk. Curley joined her, lapping milk. He seemed to be welcoming her—a prospective new American cat friend. She didn't flare up at him or otherwise show mistrust.

Where had she come from? Perhaps something had panicked her, and she had reached us after a wild flight. Maybe, I told myself hopefully, with her hunger gone, she will get reoriented and go back to her real home. On the ridge across the ravine lived a young couple with eleven cats and no dogs. She might belong to them. I put her in the car and drove over to find out.

They recognized her at once. A cat in their family looked like her only a little smaller. A few evenings past they had heard a car stop on Cavedale Road below their place and a car door slammed. At the time they thought that someone coming to visit them had overshot their drive. The car took off again burning rubber. The following day these two cats walked in hungry.

They were a brother and sister pair. Gessino, the young man of the place, and I talked it over. We concluded that the two might want to stay together until we could find them a home, so I left the female. That afternoon she showed up again in our carport. Gessino told me later that their top female drove her off, but the brother stayed.

Anyhow she seemed to like our place although we didn't let her in the house with the other cats and fed her in the patio. She got along with Tang and Si and Curley. Curley was happy again; he had another American cat friend.

Gessino and I tried to find homes for these strays. But the "come-and-get-it" column in the local paper didn't bring us any satisfactory results. We were faced with turning them over to the local SPCA which meant the pound and the decompression chamber.

We put off doing anything, and the longer that little tabby-splotched character stayed with us the more attached to her we became. The same thing was happening to Gessino and Pat, his friend. So, they kept the brother, making an even dozen felines for them. We kept the sister. She became our number four cat, Missy by name.

She was gentle, affectionate, clean and adaptable. She seemed completely house-oriented. She knew about radios, TVs and vacuum cleaners. She didn't know about typewriters. Obviously, she hadn't lived in a writing family. She examined both my machine and Ruth's with great feline care.

One of her traits puzzled us. She checked out every car and its occupants that came to our place. As Ruth said, "She seemed to be looking for the car and/or people she knew—the people who threw her and her brother away."

In the fall we had her spayed. She and our other cats never really played together but they were friendly. As winter approached she became a great hunter. Almost any time, day or night, we were likely to find her eating some catch, gopher, rat, vole or ground squirrel on the patio lawn. She roamed farther and farther in search of game but always returned. Perhaps she checked out newcomers in the neighborhood in her endless search for the people she had known. She checked out some trigger-happy kids shooting rabbits and they shot her.

Curley had lost an American cat friend again. He and the Siamese got on better that winter. The people at the head of the ravine had an unneutered tom who came over hoping to jump Si or Tang. Curley fought him. He became a defender of the Siamese.

The following summer Si was killed by a rattlesnake. I mistook the sound of a snarl, as Si came through the flexport, as a run-in with that feral tomcat. I thought the evidence of injury was the result of that supposed fight, and put off doing anything about it until too late.

Tang felt the loss of Si most and we replaced him with a two-month-old pet shop Siamese kitten. Ruth named him Mao Tse-tung. Tang let the kitten play with his tail the first day. Mao was a high point in Curley's life: now he had a Siamese playmate.

The big, gallumping red tabby treated Mao as gently as any mother could her kitten. The pet shop product had never been on the ground before he came to us. Curley took him in hand, taught him tree-climbing and country lore. He fought the feral tomcat to protect his kitten.

That November another cat came to live with us. Her markings were very much like the Missy we had lost, but this young cat was a Manx. To me she became Missy Manx. We felt that she and Mao were about the same age. They got along well together, playing like kittens. Very often she started the action. Sometimes if Mao didn't respond when she wanted to play, she would bite his balls. That got results but usually a fight rather than a game.

Again Curley was left out of the games. He wanted to play with Missy but the little Manx was afraid of his size. Ruth said that Curley was like Lenny in Steinbeck's *Of Mice and Men*. He'd jump her and she'd squall. Curley would look puzzled, "I only wanted to play." And Mao would come to her defense. He was good-natured about it; he's a good-natured cat, but he made it clear to Curley that the tabby must be careful with Missy Manx. This perplexed Curley, even hurt his feelings, and perhaps even began a resentful feeling toward the Siamese. Perhaps it was a feeling that festered and was expressed later.

In the spring I took Missy Manx to be spayed and when I went to pick her up two days later, I took Mao to be neutered. His cage was next to hers. I opened her cage door and held him so the two could sniff noses. The nose contact continued for more than a minute. Maybe Missy did all the communicating, "Let me tell you about my operation," and Mao let her have her say. I wish I knew what they said to each other.

Missy Manx was in excellent condition when I brought her home. Her incision didn't seem to bother her at all. By comparison Mao's operation was minor. Unlike Si he had a good "trip" on the anesthetic and was ready to come home by two o'clock in the afternoon. Even the doctor's wife, his assistant in surgery, was amazed at Mao's rapid comeback.

Not long after Missy and Mao had their operations another calico cat appeared. Later we discovered that she was the reason Missy had come to us months before. The Manx, as a kitten, had been a replacement for the neighbor's calico that had died. After school started, a calico kitten had followed the neighbor's two boys home from the school bus stop. The neighbor family had accepted the kitten and Missy Manx walked out.

Perhaps Missy had said to herself, "There ain't enough grub here for one cat, let alone two. I'm going to find a better home."

True to their feline beliefs, the neighbors hadn't had the calico spayed and she was in heat. In search of a male she visited our cats, saw Mao and fell for him. She rubbed against him, washed him, hugged him, rolled in front of him and put her rear end up in his face. Mao thought she was wonderful but there was nothing he could do about it. Missy Manx caught them together, attacked the calico and drove her home. When she returned from the chase, she lashed out at Mao. In spite of the jealous Missy, the romance between the neutered Mao and the calico continued. Like a good soap opera the lovers met in the woods between their respective homes. Calico didn't dare come see him because of the jealous Missy. Mao didn't dare go over to her place because of strange people and a big dog. They met and smooched and sat on adjacent rocks in silent communion. Mao's body still produced hormones but he couldn't function as a tomcat. In time, a stray tom showed up and satisfied the calico's demands. That didn't affect the romance. She and Mao continued to meet near the property line in the woods.

When the kittens came, Mao, older and tougher now, had discovered he could bluff the neighbor's big dog. He went to visit the new family. The neighbor learned another lesson about cats: male cats don't kill kittens. Maybe strange hungry feral males do but not well-fed, neutered males.

Although Mao was only a proxy father of the calico's kittens, he treated them as if they were his own. Every day he paid them a visit, and watched them play. The neighbor's wife was amazed at this "cute" little family scene.

Romance and the Neutered Cat   115

That spring we acquired new tenants, a young couple with two spayed female cats. Mao was immediately friendly with them. Missy Manx attacked them at every opportunity, probably because of Mao's attention to the new cat tenants. If Mao happened to be around he stopped the quarrel by placing himself between the antagonists.

Curley tried to play with them but he usually reverted to his longer tomcat conditioning and the young spays squalled. Mao broke up such quarrels too. Each time the red tabby seemed surprised and puzzled. He didn't lash back. Each time the expression on Mao's face seemed friendly, as if trying to communicate a message, "Cut it out, will you? Leave my girls alone."

On the surface Curley didn't seem to resent this interference. Yet such occurences might have been the basis for the red tabby acquiring a malicious streak. After all, Curley had suffered hunger, abandonment, danger, while Mao had experienced none of these. Besides, Mao was a Siamese.

At this time Tang was still alive and number one cat. He was *my* cat and my lap was his to sleep on whenever he felt like it. Curley, apparently man-oriented, recognized Tang's priority. That too was a point of resentment: those uppity Siamese.

Our tenants also acquired a Siamese kitten, Buckwheat. Curley accepted him and played with him. Mao liked the kitten too. He often brought Buckwheat up to play on the lawn and in the shop and carport. After romping for awhile the two would disappear down to the apartment. In a few minutes Mao would return alone and set off across the field on some business of his own. Whether Mao sensed that Buckwheat was tired and needed rest, or just didn't want him tagging along when he went hunting, I don't know. Curley didn't treat the kitten with the same consideration Mao showed him. Maybe Mao sensed that Buckwheat was ill. Early that fall he died of a malady the vet diagnosed as congenital. Later the two older cats, the two spayed females, died similarly.

I don't suppose our Missy Manx felt any sorrow at their passing; if a cat can feel sorrow. They had threatened her position. Mao and Curley missed them, even if they didn't quite understand, as we humans did, what had really happened.

As for Tang, he was too old to care much for anything but my lap, the fire in the fireplace and a shining sun.

11

Fun and Games in Feline Society

Our New York red tabbies played together as kittens and as grown cats. Sometimes their games turned serious and a real fight developed which we had to break up. Eventually they came up with a unique way of ending a game peacefully. When they reached a stand-off, the cat wanting to call a halt swept a paw slowly down in front of the other's nose. Claws were sheathed. The paw didn't appear to touch the other cat. After a couple of passes, the cat being stroked would sneeze and the game was over.

I saw this happen many times and puzzled about the action. There didn't seem to be any threat evident in the sweeping paw. Why the sneeze? Then I realized that the sweeping paw passed just close enough to the other cat's nose so that the fine hair between the pads tickled. A few such passes and the tickling brought on the sneeze. I was never sure the cats knew what they were doing or were aware of the results.

A catnip binge could turn a playful gesture into a brawl. I

could only guess that was how a fight started when we were living in our second place in Putnam County. Our red tabbies were Leo IV and Timmy. One hot summer morning I heard a quarrel start on the garden path. I suspected one of the combatants was ours and a neighborhood cat.

From our window I saw yellow bodies spinning, yellow hair flying and the country calm torn by furious screams. The battlers broke and one headed up the slope toward the house. It was Timmy. Right behind him, to my astonishment, came his mother Penny, who lived a couple hundred yards up the drive. Tim bounded across this driveway, but the old lady—close to ten years old at the time—gained on him. As he leaped up the steps to the lawn she caught him. Again they tangled. Then Leo showed up, all eighteen pounds of him, like the cavalry full gallop across the grass. He reached the action just as Timmy broke free again and landed on Penny. That knocked all the fight out of her and Timmy escaped to the house.

Leo and his mother squared off at each other, hurling foul cat epithets. Penny didn't dare attack Leo because of his size and she couldn't retire for fear he'd jump her. Both cats were panting. Finally Leo walked deliberately over to the shade of a forsythia bush. He was still close enough to keep Penny pinned down: he in the shade, she in the blistering sun. I don't know how long he would have punished the old girl if I hadn't taken pity on her. As soon as I started down the steps to the lawn, Leo came to meet me, probably expecting praise. I picked him up and took him to the house, allowing Penny to make her getaway.

Penny was always feisty but this was the first time I had ever known her to attack one of her own offspring. The cause baffled me. Maybe she and Timmy had met at the catnip "bar" in the garden. Maybe she'd had a nibble too many and picked on Tim because he was neutered. Then again, perhaps he had over "nipped" and made some crack about the generation gap.

Why did Leo come to Timmy's defense? Maybe he felt that Timmy, whom he'd raised from the age of ten weeks, was his kitten and he was being protective. That was the only time I ever saw Leo IV in a real fight. His weight made other cats respectful and he was a peaceful, friendly character.

Out here in California, Timmy initiated our first Siamese, Tiki, into the family. The second spring after he came to live with us, the friends who owned his parents promised us another male kitten. Some factor in the genes of the litter caused the males to die within a few days.

One of the females in the litter was a timid little character and our friends wanted us to take her. I'd had doubts about taking a Siamese cat in the first place and double doubts about accepting a female Siamese. I realized how difficult it is to find a good home for a sensitive cat and our friends thought we were the right people for her. She became Number Three cat in our family, named Topsy.

Timmy was growing old and didn't pay too much attention to her. If she took liberties with his tail, as kittens will, he slapped her lightly. Tiki accepted her in a big-brotherly fashion and she adored him. She learned her conduct in the family from him rather than Tim perhaps because he was Siamese.

The summer Tiki was killed, Anne decided to give me a kitten for my birthday. The friends who had given us Tiki and Topsy no longer raised kittens. However, across the street from their place, a "barn" cat had littered that spring, a mixed batch, and one of them was an orange-yellow tabby. They were ready to wean and Anne liked the idea of returning to ginger cats again, so she spoke for the orange tabby.

The day before she planned to take him, he was killed by a dog. In the same litter was a black-and-white brother—white lower jaw and white nose markings, a white shirt front, white mittens and white boots. Anne fancied him and brought him home. She called him Charlie. Later, to distinguish him from a neighbor named Charlie, his name was lengthened to Charles Addams, but he was seldom called anything but Charles or Charlie.

His mother had been ginger-colored so he showed no fear of Timmy. Although Tim had battled the neighbor's black-

and-white cat, Blackie, he was old and mellow enough to accept Charlie without much fuss. Perhaps he was even aware, somehow, of Charlie's orange-yellow parentage.

With Topsy it was different. She had accepted Timmy, a non-Siamese, because Tiki accepted him. Tim was still Number One cat to her, but she made it plain that as Number Two she was not welcoming any non-Siamese into the family. Charlie had a built-in fear of Siamese. Our friend's Siamese used to cross the street and beat up on the older cats where he was born. For a few nights Ruth let him sleep with her and during the day we were careful that Topsy didn't corner him. After a couple of weeks, Charlie learned to keep out of her way, and adapted himself to the family routine.

One night we heard a scream and scrambling out on the deck. I went out to check and found Topsy on the railing and Charlie lying on the ground below crying. When I picked him up I felt that his hindlegs or back had been injured. We suspected that he had been parading on the railing, and Topsy, seeing a chance to get at him, had knocked him off. Normally a kitten can fall the distance he had without getting hurt. But directly below the railing was a sandbox I had built for Anne. I concluded that Charlie had landed on his back on the side of it.

We were never able to find out how badly he was injured. Our vet was on vacation. We took him to another who had us leave him to be X-rayed. When I picked him up, I was shown an X-ray film and told there was nothing broken. We were advised to keep him immobile until he recovered. How do you keep a kitten immobilized? I was never sure the X-ray shown me had been taken of Charlie.

I fixed him a special cage, litterbox and food dishes. He showed little improvement and after a couple of weeks we felt that his struggles to get out were worse for him than movement if free. He'd just have to live with his injury. We let him loose.

Topsy still tried to get at him whenever she could. It looked as if we would never be able to have another cat as long as she was around. We even talked of giving her away. After some lusty whacking, she seemed to get the message that Charlie was part of the family and she had better accept him. By mid-winter Anne took a picture of Tim, Topsy and Charlie sleeping together.

Because of his injury Charlie wasn't neutered until he was almost a year old. At that time I was afraid the late operation might make him less of a hunter. Quite the contrary. He became a great hunter, but seldom ate what he caught. It was as if he felt that having climbed the social ladder from barn cat to house cat, the eating of his catches would somehow declass him.

As the threats from Topsy diminished, he began to make the most of his house privileges. He was never a lap cat, but he seemed to luxuriate on bed, couch, pillow or cushion. He could look around from such a spot with a hauteur the equal of any snooty Siamese, as if to say, "I've got it made! Here I am, a barn cat, allowed to sleep on this soft place in this nice warm house."

After Timmy's heart gave out on him, Topsy was Number One cat. Tang hadn't been inducted into our household cat protocol during his formative months, but he was a Siamese. The odd member was our "rags-to-riches" barn cat with an injury that still bothered him at times.

Topsy never really defined her top cat role. She deferred to Tang when it came to laps. My lap had become his. She took Ruth's. Charlie didn't compete there. At the food dishes Tang gave way to Charles and Topsy, and in most instances, Topsy gave way to the black-and-white, perhaps because he just barged in and began to eat, his big head taking up all the space in the first dish put down. He might have given way to the Siamese if they had asserted themselves—their royalty status. But Tang preferred horsemeat fed to him on a piece of paper—he'd been conditioned to that—and he rarely ate canned food. That left Topsy the second food dish.

When the family ate, both Topsy and Charlie teased silently for tidbits. Our first six red tabbies had behaved that way, and Timmy, the last of them, had passed this training on to Topsy and the black-and-white. Tang teased loudly and imperiously, and I was never able to break him of the habit.

The possibility that the Siamese and Charlie would come to blows worried me. One night I was awakened by an uproar in the kitchen. When I went to investigate I found tufts of grey cat fur on the floor. We had no grey cats.

A few nights later at bed time I noticed Topsy had curled up on the seat of my chair at the end of the dining table. In this first house of ours here in California, that put her just above the last cat entrance.

Weeks later a brown tabby appeared in the neighborhood. Eventually it learned to negotiate the entrance routine our cats used. Again a brawl awakened me. Same results—cat fur not belonging to our cats all over the kitchen.

I figured out the scenario: when the stranger flipped up the outside screen panel he alerted Topsy on my chair. When the interloper came through the second opening she dropped on him, all four feet clawing. The stray must have thought he'd been hit by a buzz saw and fled, never to return, leaving behind a floor covered with tabby tufts. Topsy never made the mistake of jumping Tang or Charlie.

When walk time came around, friction sometimes developed between the three cats. Tang never objected to Topsy going, but if Charlie had a head start, he might refuse to go. He'd sit and sulk.

Charles never showed priority feelings. If Tang held back, he'd slow up and call to him, trying to get him to come along. We always felt that Topsy's main interest in these walks stemmed from her tendency to be constipated. Walks in the woods excited her and made her bowels move. Of course this slowed her up. If Tang were along, he was quite willing to leave her behind. But not Charlie. He would hold back, making calling sounds perhaps urging us to wait up or Topsy to hurry.

She was one of the few cats I've known who didn't cover her scat outdoors. After digging an elaborate hole and using it, she'd walk away. Tang never did anything about it. If Charles were around, he would cover it carefully.

Tang probably recognized Topsy as Siamese, female, and Number One cat in the household—in that order. He had grown up among Siamese. They were all he knew as a kitten. In later years, he always showed a preference for Siamese newcomers over other breeds. With Topsy there might have been a difference. She accepted Tang because he replaced Tiki whom she adored. There might have been a bit of maternal feeling in her attitude.

One time I took Tang to the vet to have his teeth checked. We had been feeding him chicken necks, which were supposed to be safe and which gave his teeth something to work on, but he developed trouble eating. On the way he complained. I felt that his protest was his old fear of being given away, so I talked to him and explained what the whole trip was about.

He behaved well at the vet's. He let the doctor examine his mouth. A piece of bone had wedged between two teeth, setting up infection and decay. The vet gave him a small shot of some form of sodium pentothal, leaving the needle in the vein so that the amount could be adjusted to keep him anesthetized. I held Tang on the table and felt him lose consciousness at the first touch of the drug. The doctor removed the bone fragment, treated the infected gums, withdrew the needle and I brought Tang home.

He was in a very wobbly state when I lifted him out of the carrier in the family room, staggering about trying to recognize his surroundings as well as control his actions. Meanwhile, Topsy sat watching him on the bench along one side of the room.

I was preoccupied with Tang and didn't notice her immediately. When I did, I became aware of the expression on her face as she watched his fumbling, unsteady movements. She didn't appear frightened. Rather, she looked more like a little old lady, a doting mother, who watches her favorite son come home bombed out of his skull for the first time. After a few minutes, she got off the bench and left the house.

This happened mid-morning. She didn't show up for her supper. She didn't come in at sleep time. Ruth was away and I had to do the cat check. I called her evening and morning, but she didn't come. I began to worry.

When she hadn't shown up by the next evening, I got Tang and Charlie and we went looking for her. We found her down by the pumphouse, sitting on her brisket, paws folded, as if this had become her new home. She was quite all right, but it took a lot of coaxing to get her to return to the house. Once we had induced her to come she was soon her old self again. Maybe she forgave Tang for "tying-one-on" before the sun was over the yardarm, or maybe she realized that it wasn't the house and me who were responsible for the condition he had been in.

Tang had always shown a grudging acceptance of Charles. After Topsy was gone, he became friends with the black-and-white. No more brawls. They even played together. In the house Tang chased Charlie. Outdoors, Charlie chased Tang. They ran with the tail-arched, bouncing gait of kittens. At times Charles would come into the house and make "murrp-ing" sounds at Tang, calling him to come out and play. And Charles continued to bring home his catches for Tang to eat, while he blissfully ate canned cat food.

There came a time when Charles developed tooth trouble. I made an appointment for him at the vet, put him in the carrier and loaded him into the car while he howled loud enough for all the neighbors to hear. Tang heard and knew that Charlie was being taken away.

It was Ruth at home who had the real problem—Tang. After I drove off, she heard the Siamese going around outside calling loudly in a moaning, forlorn tone. Then he came in and began complaining to her. She tried to reassure him by telling him that Charlie was going to the vet to have his teeth checked. Then he went outside and called some more. The next time he came in, he went up to my desk where he could sit and look down the drive. As time passed and no Charles came home, he hunted up Ruth again and complained.

She repeated her story about Charlie's teeth and the vet. But that didn't satisfy him. He paced around complaining. Finally his carrying-on got on her nerves and she scolded him. He went to the coffee table in the family room where he could look through the kitchen in the direction of the utility room where the backdoor led to the carport, and there he sat sullenly with his paws tucked under him. The moment he heard the car on the drive he left the coffee table and was waiting to greet Charlie in the kitchen.

That was the behavior of a cat who had not always treated Charlie in a friendly way, beating down on him when he had the opportunity. A year or so later, when Charles was killed and didn't come back, Tang showed even more that he missed him.

Cynically, you might say, "He just didn't want to lose his source of rodents." I think it went much further. It's hard for me to find an interpretation that doesn't add up to cats caring for each other as well as people, and none of it has to do with a selfish interest in food or attention.

After Charlie's death we decided to get Tang a kitten to take his mind off his sorrow, if sorrow was his misery. We got a two-month old Siamese kitten. Bringing him home, we stopped at our mailbox for the mail and I found an offer from a London publisher for my first science fiction novel. We named the kitten Sci-Fi, which finally became Si.

When I opened the carrier in the family room Tang came eagerly to see what we had. Perhaps he had some notion that Charlie might climb out. At the sight of the kitten he gave a moderate hiss. The kitten hissed right back as if to say, "I've been hissed by bigger cats than you."

Tang headed for the flexport with Si right behind him. I just had time to stop the kitten from going through those plastic leaves as if he'd been doing it ever since he could crawl. There had been no such cat door where he had been born.

After being frustrated at this point, Si turned his attention to the house. As he went from room to room, he made a half-purring, half-growling sound that could be heard all over. He seemed to be saying, "Hey, all you other cats, I'm a big fierce Siamese and you'd better not mess with me!" Once he found no opposition he stopped making that sound. Later, when Ruth took him outdoors he made the same sound until he seemed satisfied that this new environment had nothing in it to threaten him.

Where Si was born the cats were accustomed to living outdoors. We thought we should keep him in until he got used to his new home. I put a litterbox in the utility room, showed it to him twice, and he never failed to use it. At first he'd let us know when he had to go. Wherever he was, couch, chair or rug, he'd let out a raucous Siamese yell. Then he'd take off across the room, down the length of the kitchen, around the refrigerator and up the utility room. Soon we'd hear him scratching in the sand.

He was from a large litter and there were many other cats in his former home. Competition for food must have been terrific.

The first evening with us Ruth put a pork chop bone on the paper where we fed cats. He grabbed it and ran into the utility room growling. She watched him. He put it down and looked around in a surprised way as if wondering, "Isn't anybody going to try to take this away from me?" Then he picked up the bone and brought it back to the paper beneath the counter.

By the second day Tang was washing him and letting him play with his tail.

Outdoors, Si proceeded to climb trees, as all kittens will, then yell because he couldn't get down. I've heard stories about mother cats showing treed kittens how to come backward down a tree trunk. I've always been somewhat skeptical. However, the first time Si got stuck up a tree, Tang behaved, if not like a mother cat, remarkably like a teacher. He looked up at the kitten crying in the branches, then climbed up to him and backed carefully and slowly down. Si watched and followed.

I wondered why Tang did this. It's easy to say "instinct."

Nonsense! Genes can't reach that far. He was a neutered male. Perhaps he had some memory of being shown how to come down a tree by some older cat when he was a kitten.

If to teach had been his intention, he proved it a little later. Live oak tree leaves have tiny thorns on their edges. Sometimes short twigs, thick with such prickly leaves, sprout on the trunks. Just beyond our patio fence stood just such a tree, growing at a sixty degree angle. On the upper side three feet of these prickly-leafed twigs grew.

Slanting trees are a temptation to cats—less work going up and less problems coming down. One afternoon Si raced up this slanting trunk. His momentum took him through the thorny leaves. But to come backwards down was a different matter. He tried and backed into the prickles. He began complaining loudly that he had been tricked and trapped. Neither Ruth nor I appreciated his predicament at the moment and let him yell. He'd learn!

Then Tang showed up and climbed the tree, picking his way through the leaf barrier. When he started backing down and came to the thorny leaves, he moved around the trunk to the underside, which was free of twigs, and backed on down, hanging by his claws. On the ground, he looked up at Si, as if to say, "See how easy that was" and walked off.

Si went on complaining. I don't know if, after a while, when Tang's lesson had had time to sink in, the kitten might have followed the instructions. Apparently Tang thought that one demonstration was enough, especially going through those prickly leaves on the way up. I wasn't enough of a scientific experimenter to wait and see. After letting Si scream a while longer I got up on a nearby rock and lifted him down.

When Si was about six months old Tang brought in a mouse and laid it down. We told him what a great hunter he was. Si came in, sniffed the mouse, and before Tang could protect it, grabbed it and dashed off growling. Tang looked surprised and perhaps a little hurt. He hadn't brought in any teaching prop for the kitten. And Tang wasn't used to having his catches stolen.

The next time he announced a catch and I praised him as usual, another mouse lay on the kitchen tile. He looked up at me with his customary expression of pride and satisfaction.

Then Si appeared. Apparently he thought this was another mouse for him. He dashed in to grab it. Tang never took his eyes off my face, but he brought a paw down on top of the kitten's head, driving his chin to the floor. The blow stopped Si so fast that his rear end flew up over his shoulders. Si backed off shaking his head, very much surprised by Tang's unkind action. The old Siamese hadn't used his claws, although it's a wonder he didn't give the kitten a "whiplash."

That spring, Si brought in his first mouse. It was still alive and I had to dispatch it. Although Tang had been used to Charlie bringing in game for him, he made no attempt to take this catch from Si. However, rather than consideration, it might have been because this was a long-tailed, big-eared variety of mouse and he didn't like them anyhow.

The next time Si brought in a catch, a vole, dead this time, and we praised him for it, Tang stole it and ate it. He liked voles. After that Si didn't bring his catches into the house, at least not the small ones. But when he caught a young rabbit he was so proud of himself that he brought it in and showed it, got his due praise and shared the meal with Tang. And I'm sure that Tang was happy with his new protégé.

That same spring, Curley joined the family. He deferred to the Siamese. For three years he accepted his outsider status exchanging it for a home with us and food regularly.

Then in the summer of '71 Si was killed by a rattlesnake. We replaced him with a two-month-old Siamese kitten we named Mao Tse-tung. Curley welcomed him eagerly: now he had a Siamese playmate. But as Mao grew, being Siamese seemed to elevate him to a superior position in the family. He and Curley remained good friends. Mao had an advantaged life from the beginning. He had always been fed and loved and protected. Curley had gone through months, maybe years—we don't know how long—of scrounging a living before he found us. That difference in their early lives might have made the difference in their characters.

I never knew Mao to "pull rank" on Curley. Yet the red tabby, I feel, resented him. Perhaps it was Mao's interference with his treatment of Missy Manx and the female cats belonging to our tenant. Maybe he waited and waited for an opportunity to even a "long score," in some way, with the younger Siamese.

The Count de Buffon is supposed to have said that the cat possesses "an innate malice and perverse disposition." That is a sweeping generalization that obviously doesn't fit all cats, but one particular spring night Curley came close to measuring up to first-rate human animal maliciousness.

After Tang died, Curley preempted my lap. Any time during every twenty-four hours that it is available and he is present, he is on it. I have to forcibly remove him if I'm tired of holding him, and he takes my action with a very injured air. If another cat should happen to be on my lap, and he comes in, he will try to crowd it off, or sulk. If one of the other cats asks to share my lap while he's on it, he tries to bat the other feline away.

Mao and he seldom came into conflict over laps because Mao considered Ruth's lap his, while mine was Curley's. If no laps were available the cats had various other sleep places: special chairs, couch cushions, a serape folded the length of an ottoman, or on a plum-colored wool blanket which we used as a cover if either of us wished to nap in the family room.

Almost every evening, at this time, I occupied a wide seat next to the front windows, facing the fireplace, while I listened to the stereo, read or watched TV. Curley would wait impatiently until I took my place and propped my feet on the coffee table, then he was up and stretched out on my legs.

On the room side of this seat was an end-table holding a tall lamp. Next to it was Ruth's recliner. Next to it stood another end-table which held the telephone and some books. Beside it was a large upholstered chair in front of which stood the ottoman with the serape folded on the top.

This particular night, Ruth had gone to the movies with a

neighbor. Curley had settled for the night on my lap while I listened to music. I could be sure the red tabby would remain on my lap until I put him off.

I paid only slight attention when Curley raised his head and looked toward the kitchen. Another cat had come in. Curley had heard dry cat food being eaten apparently; I hadn't. He continued looking in the direction of the kitchen.

The possibility of some strange feline trespassing might have aroused Curley's interest and I noticed his behavior. I looked to see what caught his attention just as Mao came to a spot on the floor between the kitchen and the family room and began washing, indicating that he'd been the cat eating and that he had finished. Normally Curley would have paid no attention to this, but he continued watching Mao.

Then I saw him glance to the upholstered chair by the ottoman. On it lay the plum-colored blanket partially folded. Curley's glance shifted back to Mao and his vigorous washing. Deliberately he got up from my lap, walked across the end-table holding the lamp, across Ruth's recliner, across the end-table with the telephone and curled up on the blanket on the chair. I watched him look briefly at Mao, then put his head down on his paws as if asleep.

Mao finished his grooming. He looked around casually, then as if his mind had already been made up, he went directly to the chair that Curley now occupied, put one front paw on the edge as if preparing to jump up. He saw the red tabby already ensconced. He looked over at me, then turned to the ottoman and got up on the serape. That didn't seem to suit him. He looked once more at Curley before jumping over to Ruth's recliner. He turned around several times in the seat. Then he came over to the wide arm of my seat and made several "merrping" sounds at me. I patted my lap but he rejected it and looked back at Curley on the wool blanket. The red tabby's head was up now watching. Mao got down and went outdoors again.

Curley looked after him. Had he known that while Mao was grooming himself he had in mind occupying the wool blanket for a nap? Normally Curley stayed on my lap. Did he intentionally get off and beat Mao to the blanket? Had he been playing a joke? Did he just want to stir up a little argument, see how far he could push Mao? Or was he getting back at the "privileged" Siamese?

I've seen humans play malicious little tricks like Curley pulled.

12

Wildlife and the Feral Cat

Perhaps it's to avoid giving cats the edge on "man's best friend," the dog, that the two are linked together: feral dogs and cats. The only similarity is that both species are domestic animals that, because of circumstances, have gone wild.

Feral dogs form packs, even dogs with homes join in and they destroy livestock and wildlife. They become a threat to humans. The feral cat makes its principal prey the small destructive rodents, gophers, mice, voles, ground squirrels and, to a smaller degree than usually assumed—birds. The feral cat kills no more birds than the predator hawk or owl. Feral cats will venture in among farm fowl and kill baby chicks and ducklings. In general, the feral cat is good for the ecological system. However, it is still a domesticated animal forced to go wild, forced to live a life that it is basically not meant for.

The feral cat really becomes a nuisance when it tries to move back into a domestic situation: the feral tomcat looking for a home, food and a female in heat.

Shortly after we took Curley in we were plagued by a real feral tomcat. He was a beautiful cream-colored specimen, probably the victim of abandonment on some back road. He tried to move in on us, but Curley fought him off. I had to break up many battles. In spite of being neutered, Curley defended his new territory.

To Gessino and Pat who lived across the ravine with their household of cats, he became a terror. They had a large neutered male, a Maltese named Fox, and he was a fighter. He was considerably older than Curley and no match for a young feral stray.

They decided that something had to be done. Gessino, a gentle person, considered shooting this cat we had come to call Creamy. But when he got him in the sights of his rifle, he couldn't pull the trigger. We discussed trapping him. The cage I had used to transport the two Siamese at the time of the fire, had been constructed originally to catch a stray cat. I loaned it to Gessino. He set it and caught Creamy.

Now, what to do with him? We had looked into the "animal control" setup in the county of Sonoma. It ran the "pound" where unwanted kittens, cats and dogs were taken. Technically they were kept for seventy-two hours to give owners of lost animals a chance to claim them, or anyone wanting a pet to come get one. After this period of grace, the captive could be sold or given to a laboratory for research or be destroyed in the "decompression chamber."

Although I know a laboratory which takes wonderful care of the cats it uses, I don't like the idea. Creamy was hardly a laboratory type. The possibility of his being put to death in a "decompression chamber" was another matter.

This device came out of the space program. One of the routines in the training of astronauts was to put them in a sealed chamber, then reduce the oxygen to simulate the elevation of the chamber to 30,000 feet. This took thirty minutes. The removal of the oxygen at this elevation was not lethal and when the trainee came out he reported the sensation of gently going to sleep.

The assumption followed that if small animals were put in such a chamber and the oxygen reduced to simulate an elevation of 60,000 feet, the animal would peacefully go to sleep and not awaken. A fine, humane idea. The catch was, that to work humanely, the time it took the chamber to reach this simulated 60,000 feet had to be at least sixty minutes.

What pound had that kind of time to spend destroying the many small animals it got every day? So attendants simply pushed up the arrival at 60,000 feet in a shorter time. Instead of going peacefully to sleep the inner organs of the small animals exploded. Some were still alive, although dying, when removed from the chamber.

Gessino couldn't accept this end for Creamy any more than he could pull the trigger of his rifle. So he took him forty miles into wild country and turned him loose. He hoped to give him a fighting chance to survive, live off the land like wildlife. He hoped that Creamy was far enough from a community such as ours that he would do no more terrorizing of domestic cats.

"When I let him out of the cage," Gessino told me, "he ran about twenty feet, then stopped and looked back at me. He seemed puzzled by what was happening to him." It is easy to think that what our friend did was wrong. The alternative was for him to do what I did with the little wild female kitten. He could have taken Creamy to the vet and have him euthanized. But that cost money and those young people didn't have that kind of money.

A year or so later, a local spay and neutering clinic was established. It made possible the handling of roaming, unneutered tomcats who can become as much of a nuisance as the feral kind.

One such tomcat belonged to the neighbor who didn't believe in neutering toms or spaying females, or feeding any of his cats more than a bit of milk. This one came to our place looking for food. Curley fought him. Curley's deformed ear got him into trouble. Because of its curled and tightened shape, he couldn't lay it back in a fight like a cat's normal ear.

The roaming tom hooked it. The scratch became infected, requiring trips to the vet, expense and a lot of misery for our red tabby.

We complained to this neighbor, and finally, offering to pay half of the cost, got him to consent to have his cat neutered. Of course this didn't stop the trouble. Even after neutering the hormone production continues for months before the cat loses its desire to roam. So this cat went right on being a nuisance around our place and a menace to our cats.

Anne loaned me a cage trap she used to catch strays where she lived. I set it and almost immediately caught this feline whose body still produced enough hormones to make him troublesome. Now, what should I do? If I confronted the neighbor with his cat in my trap I would have gotten no satisfaction from him. After all, he'd gone through with the neutering, hadn't he? I paid half the cost, finally, and I still wasn't satisfied.

I could have turned this cat in to the animal control people and let him face the horrors of the pound. I could have taken him to our vet and had him euthanized. This cat and his harrassment of ours had been responsible for my thinking that our Si had been clawed in a fight when in fact he had been bitten by a rattlesnake. This same cat attacked and injured Mao who replaced Si.

In desperation, I did something I don't believe in doing, and actually it should never have to be done if people neutered and spayed their cats the way they should. I took this cat into dairy country and freed him near a pond and a thriving dairy farm. I rationalized that there he would have a chance to become a useful cat around the place.

But I can assure you I wasn't happy about what I did.

A year or so later a similar situation developed with the tomcat of a family on Cavedale Road. They had their female spayed. The man's machismo wouldn't let the tom be neutered. Eventually he began roaming. He visited the unspayed female of our neighbor living at the top of the ravine. On his way back from those visits he stopped at our place. Curley fought him. He terrorized Mao. He learned to negotiate the flexport and ate our cats' food. I finally prevailed upon these people to have him neutered. I trapped him and, taking the neighbor's wife along, took him to the clinic and had the job done.

Habit and the continued production of hormones still brought him around. Periodically he made visits to the place at the top of the ravine. On the way back he stopped off at our place for a snack. He still fought Curley and Mao.

One night the following January, Mao came dashing into the house—a warning that the stray was outside. I went out and told him to go home. A light rain had begun. He knew me. He wasn't really scared of me. I chased him out of the carport. He sat in the drizzle and yowled forlornly as if pleading with me to let him come in out of the rain and get a bite to eat. I firmly told him to go home. Finally he sat out down the drive.

That night the hormones in his system had tapered off. He never came back. When I drive past his home I occasionally see him, now content to stay around the house. I've inquired about him from the wife and she says, "He's a very friendly homebody—really a very nice cat." I'm sure he is but he would be a nicer cat had they had him neutered at the proper age.

Living in the country we are inevitably on the edge of some wildlife habitat. Our cats have been able to cope with the inhabitants. I have always felt that they know all the local wildlife residents and there is a détente between them.

The summer in Putnam County when we kept the cat-boarder, Orphy, I was awakened one morning by an unusual thumping sound. We were living in our first cottage. A double-decker was the only bed for two that our bedroom would hold. I slept in the top bunk which placed me at eye-level with the window overlooking the driveway beyond the terrace, and the down-sloping field of alfalfa that stretched to our stone wall boundary.

I didn't locate the source of the thumping at once. In the drive, opposite the window, Orphy sat vigorously washing his cream-colored fur. The thumping sound didn't bother him, but it continued. I sat up to get a better look. There, coming up the field toward him were two deer, a buck and a doe. They moved like a pair of dancers, abreast, in step, stamping each front foot in unison. I cautiously awakened Ruth so that she could see the show.

Orphy never stopped slurping to give the stompers a look. On they came. Ruth and I got out of bed and rested our elbows on the window ledge watching. The deer came up to within three or four yards of the drive. Then the little buck seemed to sense his audience in the window and the dance ended. The two backed slowly off, turned and ambled across the field and over the stone wall into the woods. Orphy slumped down on his spine to wash his belly. Ruth and I went back to bed.

Actually the wildlife around us has never been as much a problem as the livestock of neighbors. The family at the top of the ravine presented us with more trouble with their goats and fighting cocks. The cocks weren't let loose but the hens and goats were. Our yard isn't fenced to keep them out and they did considerable damage.

One day, after driving off the goats which were stripping bark from our madrone trees, I asked a lawyer friend what could be done about such depredations. He told me I had a right to shoot the trespassing goats and chickens—if I owned a gun. Of course, the neighbor could retaliate by shooting my cats if they strayed on what he considered his property. I could sue, but civil suits are a drag. Besides, it was doubtful if the guy had money to pay damages if I won.

"It's too bad," my friend said, "that something couldn't just happen to his roaming stock." Then he slapped his forehead. "What am I saying! I'm an officer of the court. I shouldn't be suggesting anything like that to you."

We laughed and I returned home with the problem unsolved. Two days later while working at my desk, I leaned back and looked out our west windows. There on the side of the huge lava boulders not ten feet from the wall lay an animal curled up asleep. It look somewhat like a cat from the distance, but not one of ours—much like an Abyssinian cat. I called down to Ruth, "Is that an Abyssinian cat on those rocks?"

She yelled back," "Abyssinian nothing! That's a fox."

A pair had moved beneath the huge boulder that lay on the down slope just below the rocks near the house. An opening beneath made room for a comfortable den. The pair had four kits. We hoped these foxes would take care of some of the neighbor's trespassing hens. They did, but not in any substantial number.

I'm sure our cats knew about these new tenants but there seemed to be no confrontation between the two species. Curley and Mao outweighted the adult foxes by several pounds.

A responsible neighbor on the other side of us also had chickens but kept them penned up. I warned them about foxes. One night however their youngster forgot to shut the chicken coop and a hen was stolen. The wife called me in the morning. "Paul, you've got to keep your foxes shut up." She was joking.

Her husband had read *Never Cry Wolf*, and learned how wolves mark their territories. He decided to put his chicken coop and chicken run out of bounds. He drank a six-pack of beer and marked the area around the yard. He lost no more chickens to foxes.

They moved from beneath our rock but remained in the area drinking from the horse-trough, leaving their scats in the drive. Occasionally we saw them in the woods eating manzanita berries.

One April morning the following spring, I saw one of the foxes come from the sunbathing side of our patio, cross the small lawn to an oak tree, raise his leg, and continue around the front of the house.

The next day I saw Curley come from the direction of the shop and cruise about, reading messages. He stopped at the oak tree, sniffed, then sprayed over the sign left by the fox.

A morning or so later, when I came out to the family room, I found Ruth chortling to herself. She had just seen Curley squatting in the mat of white violets that carpeted the area between the house and the lava boulders. The fox showed up, charged him, and Curley, taken by surprise, raced up around the house to the deck.

We don't know how many encounters the cats and foxes had. Their habitats overlapped. Maybe they reached a stand-off. The foxes lived off birds, berries, rodents and the wild chickens.

About six weeks after the fox chased Curley, I sat by the window overlooking the boulders and the valley at dusk. My feet were propped up on the coffee table and Curley stretched full length on my legs.

One of the foxes came up from the lower side of the house, and started to follow the top of the retaining wall to the bed of white violets. Curley let out a scream and charged down to the window. The fox whirled and charged across the violets to meet him. They came nose to nose at the glass wall, eyeballing each other in fury, hair bristling from head to tail tips. The fox turned and fled from sight over the edge of the lava boulders. Curley, still bristling, resumed his place on my legs.

The family at the top of the ravine had moved away, taking goats, fighting cocks and troublesome tomcats, abandoning a pregnant female cat to the new owner. The neighborhood cats now lived in comparative peace in a wildlife habitat of fox, raccoon, skunk, civet cat, perhaps even a bobcat, but the peace can be broken.

Another close neighbor had a few ducks and geese. She told me her ducks had been wiped out and now the predator was eating the geese eggs. I might have advised, "Call the animal control and let them handle the problem." Sometimes you can be lucky and such an obvious solution will pay off. More often you'll find yourself in a *Catch 22* situation.

She and I tried to determine the predator. The terrain is brushy, hilly and wild. The ducks were stolen from a pen and the eggs eaten were inside a coop within a pen. That ruled out feral dogs and foxes, and narrowed the culprit or culprits to feral cats and other climbing predators.

I offered to set my cage trap in the goose pen and see what we might catch. It was baited with cat food and an egg on Wednesday evening, but not until Sunday night was it touched. Monday morning our neighbor called to say we had caught a big raccoon.

I offered to dispose of it for her. But that wasn't as easy as it sounds. If I had had a gun and an itchy trigger finger, the solution would have been simple. Shoot it. I wouldn't have had trouble with the law, and probably only incurred a moderate protest from some of the other neighbors.

However, I felt that animals have some rights. The neighborhood had encroached upon the raccoon's territory, and our neighbor's ducks and geese eggs must have seemed fair prey. There was another problem. I didn't know its sex. It was just a bundle of angry fur in a cage. If it were male, it could have been removed without creating a serious problem. If it were a pregnant female, removal from the neighborhood would probably be all right. If it had young in some nearby den or nest, either removal from the area or killing it would produce a situation which, I for one, didn't want to face. I called the *Animal Control Agency* and asked their help.

"It's a wild animal," I was told, "and the county only authorizes us to handle domestic animals—dogs and cats."

The officer switched me over to the *Predator Control Agency*. The officer for that facility said, "It wasn't caught in one of our traps and we can't touch it."

When I pointed out the problem about sex, I was told, "Just turn it over and examine it." I looked at the snarling, masked face, and the clawed hands tearing at the mesh of the cage and asked the officer to come do that himself. The answer was the same—it wasn't caught in one of their traps—they couldn't touch it.

My next call was to the *county humane society*. I was told bluntly that they couldn't handle it at all. When I called the regional office of the *State Fish and Game Department* I thought I might be getting somewhere. They told me I could just go out and release it anywhere.

Sure, I could take it fifteen or twenty miles away and free it to prey upon some other person's ducks or chickens, fruit or whatever food was available.

I called our county supervisor. His office contacted the ranger at a nearby state park and asked if they would accept a raccoon. They said they'd be happy to have it.

By this time my captive had done enough gyrating in its attempt to escape from the trap to reveal most parts of its anatomy. It was a male and I felt satisfied delivering him to the park. He loped off into his new environment, no worse for his experience than the humiliation of being caught, and taken twenty miles in the open trunk of my car exposed to the stares of people in cars following.

All in all it was a successful relocation. His rights had been recognized and maintained and he had been returned to a natural and rightful habitat.

With feral dogs and cats there is no chance for relocation. They occupy an alien habitat. That's why they're feral. They have no rights except those accorded them by sympathetic people.

Shortly after the raccoon affair, an acquaintance living in Sonoma, connected with the local spay clinic, asked to borrow my trap. Her neighborhood was being victimized by a feral tomcat. He was a beautiful red tabby, but thin, wild and hungry. It was natural that he acquired the name "Morris." The lady had tried to catch him, but wasn't able to even get close enough to touch him, let alone pet him.

He fought the cats of the area. In no time he learned to negotiate the various cat-doors, entered the houses and stole food. Being unneutered, he sprayed furniture and shrubbery.

The lady set my trap and soon caught this troublemaker.

Now, the problem of the disposal of "Morris" was far different from that of the raccoon. Morris had no rights. He had become a pariah and a menace in a normal feline habitat. If there had been an adequate facility, and someone had had the time to work with him, tame him, neuter him and make him into a domestic pet, he might have been saved. The lady already had five cats, four of them strays she had taken in. The environment was saturated with cats—saturated because of those irresponsible people who let their cats breed indiscriminately, then abandon or dump the adults and offspring wherever they can.

This lady could have called the *Animal Control Agency* and they would have picked up this domestic animal. He would have been turned over to the pound and the decompression chamber. Or she could have put cage and Morris in her car and taken him far into the country and turned him loose. What happened to him in this new and natural habitat would be "his problem."

But our situation has improved since the time Gessino had to get rid of Creamy. The lady knew that she could take this handsome red tabby to the clinic and have him put to sleep by injection.

Still, even that is a hard, painful decision and not a pleasant one to think of at night. There is a tiny straw of good feeling to cling to: the satisfaction in knowing that this beautiful cat, callously abandoned, will be "put down" painlessly.

So I helped the lady put the trap and the red tabby dubbed "Morris" in her station wagon and take him to the clinic. I talked to Dr. James Corbett, a veterinarian gentle with small animals. He didn't like what he had to do, but he had inured himself to the job, knowing that he would be giving an unterrifying death to an unwanted small creature.

Feeling safe and unthreatened in the cage, and well fed with the bait that got him there, "Morris" was quite calm. He sat on his brisket, paws folded beneath him. But any feral cat can be dangerous to handle. A sudden move, any possible threat can turn it into a snarling fury, with savage claws ready to rip and tear.

Doctor Corbett approached the trap, a syringe loaded with a tranquilizing drug ready. He moved close and thrust the needle through the mesh of the cage into the cat's hips. At the prick of the point, "Morris" let out a sharp snarl. Then he relaxed and in a couple of minutes he became completely immobilized.

Carefully, Doctor Corbett removed the orange body from the cage and laid it on the gravel. He had a second syringe loaded with a lethal dose of pentobarbital and injected it directly into the animal's heart. At the touch of the needle this time Morris was completely unconscious and in a few minutes this beautiful red tabby was dead.

If you feel the hurt that we felt, at the waste of such an act, then stop the possibility of such incidents happening. You can prevent similar deaths, and many much worse deaths to cats by making sure that spaying and neutering reduces the number of unwanted small animals. Then support adequate shelters to take care of the others.

13

And Some Go Gently into That Long Sleep

All cats miaow in the same language; all kids cry in the same language; all people, all mammals, all living beings die in the same language all over the world. Not a very profound idea. Call it fatuous if you like. It is just an obvious truth.

To consider the death of a loved one, or of a friend, or the death of oneself before being faced with the fact may seem morbid to many, and callous to some. Yet it seems to me that not until we replace a fear of death with understanding and respect, can we have a true love and appreciation of life.

It is neither morbidity nor callousness that has prompted colleges and universities to add courses on death and dying to their curricula. And these courses have large enrollments. To me it is a sign of mental maturity for a person to face up to the mortality of all living things, human and non-human—myself and my cats.

Not long ago, in an issue of the magazine *All Cats*, Professor Jim Lynch, who teaches such a course, had an article on

"Death . . . and our Cats." He referred to the book *On Death & Dying* by Dr. Elizabeth Kubler-Ross which is used to help terminally ill people face the inevitable, and for counseling those who must go through the experience with them. Dr. Kubler-Ross lists five stages in facing terminal illness and death, either for a loved one or for ourselves.

Professor Lynch finds that the loss of one's cat follows a similar pattern. First we *deny* that it can happen to us or our cat. Then we're *angered* by its happening. If it is possible, we'll *bargain*—we'll try to get concessions out of our vet or perhaps a deity. When that fails, *depression* comes. We feel sorry for ourselves and our cat. Finally we *accept* what is inevitable. And if we are lucky to have been able to handle all of these stages we will wind up with good memories of our feline companion.

Some people get hung-up on one of these stages, and never make it beyond. This can mean trouble unless it passes. Also, if more than one person is involved, each can be in different stages at the same time, resulting in misunderstandings and misery for all concerned.

Except in instances of sudden death, the dying individual, cat or person, goes through the same stages. We can't help our cat friend much because of our inability to explain to him what is happening. It is the same as it would be with a dying infant, or perhaps someone whose language we do not know. And in the long run, it is what the living must face that is more difficult than the one who is dying.

With a dying cat, we very often have to handle a feeling of guilt for some inadequacy at a crucial time. Maybe we didn't pay attention to symptoms and behavior. Maybe we let the bargaining stage go too far; let a vet continue treatment long after our friend, whose life is completely in our hands, should have been "put down."

The *Pet Pride* organization has drawn up sixteen Cat's Rights, I'm in complete agreement with all of them. However, like all such rules, they are open to interpretation by the cat owner and cat lover. There is no hundred percent sure interpretation.

To some, the care and protection of a cat means keeping it indoors at all times. For an apartment or condominium dweller in a "high density" area that's the only way a cat can be protected. Perhaps the most one can do in such an environment is to train one's cat to a leash and take it out to the park.

Cats are free spirits, some more than others, the same as people are. Some neutered cats adjust well to the confinement of an apartment but that doesn't insure their complete protection. Many times in apartment fires the cat isn't rescued. The apartment-confined cat is subject to ailments resulting from its confinement. I point this out because we have been criticized for letting our cats roam. With our country environment, it is impossible for me to confine my cats indoors while I enjoy the woods and the world outside. Our cats don't wander unprotected. We do have laws intended to protect pets but the Judeo-Christian Ethic places any non-human animal in jeopardy. The non-human animal is supposed to be inferior and any consideration for it can be taken lightly.

For a decade I "screamed" to authorities to establish the acceptance of the letter of the law that gives my cats the same protection that humans have. Why shouldn't our non-human friends live as safely as we do? Over a period of fifty years— that's half a century—we have had sixteen cats. We have four of the sixteen still. No one had produced for us the proper protocol for living and associating with a cat.

As Professor Lynch wrote, "Each of us must cope, adapt and move into life's mainstream. Yet, each does so in his or her own fashion." And in conclusion he points out, "Perhaps the pain we feel when losing our cat is indeed a positive factor in our lives."

The details surrounding the death of every one of my cats I can see today as vividly as when the tragedies happened. And each carries with it whatever involvement I had in it.

I can still see our first Leo telling his two sons with nose sniffing to lay off playing with baby chicks. They let chicks alone after that. Then that big, confident, ginger tomcat went along the stone wall and disappeared on his last trip. It was his usual going and we thought nothing of it. I never saw him alive again. A day or so later a friend came to tell us that Leo had been killed on the Post Road below their cottage.

Like the first stage set down by Dr. Kubler-Ross, my reaction was that it must be another ginger cat. I refused to accept the fact of death until I was close enough to the red tabby to see the conspicuous little kink at the tip of his thick tail. The car that hit him had driven three feet out on the shoulder of the highway.

It was then I began to realize that I must have our cats neutered. Yet, it was human animal viciousness that had killed Leo I. I cried and I buried him in the birch grove. Then Leo Secundus, Sec, left without returning. It was ten years before I was able to piece together the tragedy of his death. Again human viciousness caused his death. My guilt was in not having him neutered so he wouldn't roam.

So our third Leo, Tersh, was "fixed." Yet, one day he didn't come home; another day passed. I told myself that he couldn't possibly fall into an open well but he had. And I had to go down a thirty-foot shaft, using niches in the stone-walled sides as toe holds (I'm claustrophobic), toeing my way to water level in terror, to bring up his soaked body. Again I cried as I buried him. My guilt was in letting him roam and not making sure that neighbors kept the screen closed on their open well. (Here we have a law against open wells.)

The death of Leo IV and Leo VI came at the end of good lives. I accepted their passing with only grief.

Leo Quintus, Quin we called him, died of my own carelessness or presumption. He was not afraid of cars. The driveway to our house in Putnam County was steep and a hairpin turn at the top ended in a short stretch to the garage. Leo lay in a wheeltrack washing himself. I could have braked to a stop but I thought he'd move. He didn't. I caused his death and after thirty-five years I still find it a truth hard to live with.

Out here in California, Tiki, our first Siamese, was killed by a car on the county road he was crossing to get to Hooker

Creek Canyon to hunt. The driver of the car could have stopped. That narrow road didn't permit a speed of more than 20/25 mph. That week we had planned to leave for a trip to New Mexico but postponed it. The evening of the night Tiki was killed, he came in for his supper, but instead of going out again, he napped. At our bedtime, he awoke and left to hunt. Apparently he went straight up over the ridge and down to that narrow, one-track road between a steep cliff on one side and a drop-off on the other. Car lights blinded him.

When I circled the neighborhood hunting for Tiki and stopped at this house, the woman told me she had seen a dead cat on the road. The family was coming home from a high school graduation exercise. The driver of the car had a mean reputation. From the woman's shifty behavior, I felt that she knew what had happened, but couldn't do anything.

Later, as I mulled over the incident, I considered that if we had gone on our trip, Tiki might not have come in when he did, and napped when he did, and gone over into the canyon at just the right time to be trapped at that narrow spot in the road. Such speculation sprouts the seeds of fatalism in one's mind.

There remained Timmy and Topsy. Later we added the barn cat Charles Addams. Then Tang was given to us. One night in August, Timmy lay on the hearth in the living room of the first house I built here in California. His heart was weakening. Ruth was with him. As death drew near, he gave a cry. The other three cats came and stood around him and he died. We loved that last of what we called the Cold Spring yellows—the Putnam County, New York, red tabbies—our last tie to our first Leo.

Ten years passed and we moved Topsy and Charles Addams and Tang to our second house higher on the ridge above the Valley of the Moon. When we had to have Topsy, the home-body, euthanized, it was the same as if she had spent her entire life in an apartment.

The circumstances surrounding the death of Charlie again pulled the shadow of fate over the tragedy. For years I had left out one of the plastic leaves in the flexport as a concession to our cats. The gap let cold air in and made it easier for civet cats to negotiate the cats' door.

When October came that year, I decided to insert the absent leaf and force Tang and Charles to use the complete flexport. I knew I would have trouble. When both were out I put in the missing leaf. When they wanted to come in, both protested that their cat door had become a stone wall. I went out, picked up the nearest, pushed his head through the flexible leaves and let him finish the entrance on his own. Then I repeated the routine with the other.

Tang was the first to accept the changed situation. It was an imposition, but he went along and in a few days his goings and comings were as usual. Charles accepted when no one was around to give him a push.

One night, he came to the front door and wanted in. I went out and gave him the push-through routine. He was still asleep indoors when we went to bed. In the morning he was gone. When he decided to go out and hunt, he had negotiated the flexport without any help. I felt a moment of success. But Charlie didn't show up for his breakfast. Ruth called him but he didn't come.

We were going through a bad time: a good friend had been killed in a car accident and a day passed before I began an all-out search of the neighborhood. The neighbor at the top of the ravine told me that two nights previously, the last time we saw Charlie alive, he had been awakened at two in the morning by raccoon hounds and hunters coming over from the new road behind us and going down the ravine. He got up to see what was happening. Down the ravine, several hundred yards, he could hear hounds whining. The sound of a shot followed.

He told me that he had yelled then. Men and dogs swarmed up out of the ravine and over to the new road and away.

We never saw Charlie again. I wondered if my insertion of the missing leaf in the flexport might have held up his going out that night—held him up long enough so that he reached the ravine the moment the hounds came through to tree him and the hunters to shoot him.

I stormed to the sheriff's office about the incident, and got polite sympathy. I stormed to our supervisor. He liked cats. And there has been no raccoon hunting in the area since. When I report hearing hounds in the neighborhood to the sheriff's office, a deputy comes to investigate immediately.

Charles Addams, the black-and-white barn cat, was gone. Tang was left alone so we got him a kitten, Si, for company. In the spring Curley joined us. Summer came and brought us Missy—the white female with grey-and-black tabby splotches. The little cat who checked out cars and people as if looking for those humans who dumped her and her brother on the canyon road.

We had her spayed and given shots. She spent the winter going and coming with Tang and Si and Curley. On the third of July the following year she joined us on the deck when we ate dinner. She loved ice cream and Ruth left her a generous helping to lap up. That was the last time we saw her alive.

Missy didn't come for breakfast next morning. Ruth mentioned it. But we were planning to pick up a friend and spend the day in a park by the ocean. Missy hadn't come home by evening.

By morning I became fearful. Buzzards circled low over the new road that came up the ridge back of our house. I went to check and found a dead jackrabbit on the shoulder of the pavement. It had been shot. I returned home still bothered by Missy's absence.

Ruth and our friend sunbathed in the patio. I stood in our family room still plagued by the absence of Missy. Again I watched the buzzards swooping low. They were much farther to the left of where I'd found the jackrabbit. I put on my boots and headed through the manzanita and chemise and oak trees, zeroing in on the bank of a little ravine. Buzzards perched in a large oak and beneath it on the ground lay Missy. She had been shot eight times.

The sun scorched as I carried that small body home and buried it. My brain seethed as I called people in the neighborhood: had they heard shooting a couple of nights ago? Did their kids have guns? I called the sheriff's office. It's illegal to shoot a gun within 300 feet of anyone's house. This was Sunday. I called our supervisor. I stormed about the law enforcement setup in the county. Before that day was over the neighborhood knew that a small amount of hell had erupted over the shooting of a cat.

My unconscious let a memory surface: that Friday evening half an hour after Missy finished her ice cream; I remembered distinctly hearing a burst of shots. Missy, always looking for the people who dumped her, had gone to check these kids and their gun. They had shot her.

Now there is no more shooting in the neighborhood that isn't quickly explained and justified.

A year later, almost to the day, Si was struck by a rattlesnake. There had been no rattlers reported in the area since the brush fire of six years previous. I misread his actions and didn't get him to the vet in time to save his life.

Every time one of my cats dies I go through all the emotional stages described by Dr. Kubler-Ross. I have said repeatedly that my responsibility for my cats goes farther than it does for any human I know. Yet, given my situation and location, I still could not keep my cats indoors or caged, no matter how grand the habitat I might provide for them. It should be the part of no one to presume that he/she had the perfect living conditions for cats. And short life or long, I do not set myself up as a superior keeper of cats.

Tang lived with us the longest. After being a part of my life for eighteen years and four months he finally went gently into that long sleep. It was a peaceful sleep and for him the right sleep. And I was responsible for it when it came.

He had been a "given away" cat. During almost two decades with him I came to love him for so many qualities. He was an ideal model before my camera when I needed something alive in a picture of a finished how-to project. He required no training. I didn't have to teach him "tricks." He seemed to grasp what I wanted of him and performed it. And he'd look up at me as if to ask, "Boss, how'm I doin'? Is this what you want?"

He liked people but he was always reserved. Whenever we

had a party, he would leap lightly to my shoulders, drape himself around my neck and ride there while I passed among our guests serving wine. He never rode on the shoulders of anyone else.

Often he made it plain to me, as if I were a god-cat, that he expected me to turn on the sun when it was cloudy, stop the rain so he could hunt, build a fire in the fireplace, or turn up the thermostat, or just make a lap for him to stretch out on.

When I worked at my desk he'd drape himself across my shoulders, or curl up in my manuscript box. The sound of the fan in the electric heater beneath my desk brought him at once to find a place to curl up in the warm air stream.

On rainy days he created games to play with Ruth and the other cats. He played jokes on them too. It was probably a joke he was playing on me when, on three different occasions, I boasted to friends in his presence that "our cats seldom catch birds," that he appeared shortly with a large bird. A little persuasion from me would get him to free them and they'd fly away. Maybe he felt that my boasting about our cats should be tempered a bit.

Many times he couldn't make me understand his problems. This was probably because his problems had no answers. I felt that he and I shared sinus problems. No veterinary medicine seems to recognize that posibility. Once, I asked our vet, "How do you know when a cat has a headache?" He couldn't tell me.

Over the years, Tang's most consistent problem, at least one we could perceive, was his teeth. Before he came to us he had been conditioned to eating ground horse meat. Only on occasion would he eat commercial cat food, but seldom the dry kind. He preferred his own catches to eat, or the gophers I caught him or the prey Charlie brought him.

Year after year we had to have his inflamed gums treated or infected teeth removed. Whenever I took him in the car, I was firmly convinced that he thought I was going to give him away. For that reason I would never leave him at the clinic. When Ruth and I were abroad, out housesitter had to take him to the vet with teeth trouble and the vet insisted he be left overnight. The next morning our friend picked us up at the bus station and on the way home we stopped for Tang. I believe he was the happiest cat I've ever seen. I had miraculously come back to rescue him from that "dreadful" clinic after being away two months.

This time the vet had found that the root from one of Tang's teeth had punctured his septum, causing an infection. He had removed the tooth and we could take him home. In fact, the vet was glad to get rid of him. "Doesn't he ever stop complaining?"

"Never," I said, "when he's away from home and his people." And the vet never again urged me to leave Tang at the hospital. I put him in the carrier and took him out to the car where Ruth waited, and when she talked to him, Tang's cup of joy truly ran over that morning.

Now, for a time, Tang could enjoy his food.

He was the last to bring in a young rabbit that fall. He came from the down-ridge side of our house, head high, carrying it by the throat. It dangled limply, properly dead. Behind him at a respectful distance came Si and Curley.

When Tang reached the carport I praised him for his catch and tried to talk him into eating it in the shop instead of in his usual place beneath a table in the corner of the family room. He looked back at the two cats following him and then up at me as if to say, "You've got to be kidding. I want to eat this rabbit in peace." He pushed on through the flexport.

The others didn't follow. In a few minutes I noticed they were no longer about. I went up on the deck where I could look down among the trees below the house. There sat Si and Curley, each on a rock, watching the slope. That was where Tang had made his catch, I concluded, and the younger cats reasoned as clearly as any human could, "If the old guy isn't going to share, let's go back and pick ourselves rocks to sit on. Where there's one rabbit, there might be another."

A year or more passed. Mao came to live with us, taking the place of Si, and Missy Manx came. I noticed that Tang was having trouble again. Once I presented him with a gopher. He carried it away eagerly, then put it down and began to cry. He wanted so much to eat it. He was hungry. Yet something hurt him when he tried to tear it apart. At last he seemed to steel himself to the pain and ate the gopher.

Within a few weeks we had to feed him almost completely by hand. Either Ruth or I, it was more often Ruth, made little balls of chopped meat and let him take them from our fingers. Sometimes we could finger-feed him with other choice meat scraps.

We might have assumed that he was simply taking advantage of us. But as autumn approached he ate less and less. Biting his food seemed to hurt him. After taking a bit of chopped meat, he would suddenly run away and hide.

I took him in for an examination. What teeth he had left were sound. The vet took an X-ray of his head and reported a growth above the hard palate. Biting and chewing put pressure on this and caused severe pain. We were told it couldn't be operated on.

The feeding by hand continued whenever he'd take food. He seemed in relatively good health except for his difficulty in eating. Finally we could no longer get nourishment into him. He became weak and unsteady on his legs.

Tang was stubbornly fastidious about his toilet. He always went outdoors. With the exception of his normal territorial spraying, he never let anyone observe him dig a hole and use it. He simply would not use a litterbox in the house.

One December night he insisted on going out. I went with him. I was afraid he might be jumped by a feral cat or a roaming dog. It was rainy and the yard light turned the world beyond its range pitch black. He looked back at me once and disappeared into that blackness. I went back for a flashlight but when I returned I couldn't find him. I searched and called. Then I heard his frantic cry and saw the gleam of reflected light in his eyes, two red dots, as he came out of the night.

I knew he would stay indoors until morning now. But what about the next night and the next? He was growing weaker. After breakfast he had to go out again and I accompanied him, staying out of his sight. When he returned, instead of coming into the house with me, he chose to go up the four steps to the deck. Perhaps he hoped for sun. Below these steps was an eight-foot drop to the gravel of the car parking area. He reached the third step, then his tottering legs made him lose his footing. He would have fallen, but his sharp claws clung to the edge of the step until I got there to rescue him.

There was no hope for him continuing life safely, and Ruth agreed. Euthanasia? I had been with Topsy at the vet's when he put her to sleep. But to make Tang suffer a last trip to the clinic—I couldn't do it.

As soon as office hours permitted I called our vet and explained the situation. I asked him if he could come out and do his work here. He was a busy man, but above all a compassionate one. He promised to come out that afternoon.

It was a grey December day—the kind Tang liked to spend indoors by the fire. After lunch Ruth and I took turns holding him on our laps in front of the fireplace. We petted his taupe back. His fur was still soft but we could feel his spine and ribs since he had become so thin. We caressed his seal-brown ears and talked to him gently as we scratched his neck, feeling the vibration of a small purr. He seemed content. His blue eyes stared into the fire he loved, seeing what a cat sees in a fire. Sometimes he looked out of the window over the Valley of the Moon. We could not tell him what was coming. We kept fear away. And perhaps that lessened a little the hunger inside him.

Time passed. A few minutes after three o'clock our vet arrived. We talked a little. He examined Tang, stroked his head gently.

Waiting longer had no purpose; I held Tang in my arms in front of the fire and the fireplace he loved while the vet prepared the syringe. I pressed him close against me as the needle entered his rib cage. His head dropped to my arm at once and only a little reflex leg movement followed. I continued holding him until it ceased, two minutes perhaps, then gently passed him to Ruth who held him until his heart stopped beating.

Although misery and hurt and loss were deep in us both

Tang had gone gently into his long sleep. He would feel no more hunger that we couldn't feed, or pain that we could not help. In time the misery and hurt would go away. We still had Mao and Curley and Missy Manx. None of them would or could ever replace Tang in our lives, but they were around to be petted and talked to, and would console us.

Perhaps the lesson, if there must be a lesson, is always to have more than one cat. They will be company for each other. No matter how much we may love one, the other in its way will be equally lovable, and the lives of each and every one will add to our understanding of all the living beings in the world around us.

As Professor Lynch says, "It is our well-loved cat who gives us that rare, precious look at just how temporary and beautiful life is."

14

The Cat Who Wanted Happenings

Until a few months ago, I accepted the idea that any cat will adjust to living in an apartment. I have known several who have. So it was something of a shock when we were confronted with, as Ruth put it, "The cat who wanted 'happenings'."

Benji was his name, and he arrived the day before Halloween. A few days previously, a friend called Ruth and said her daughter, Susan, had a very unhappy Burmese in her San Francisco apartment, and wanted to find a place in the country for him.

Susan had hoped that after Benji was neutered and grew older he would become reconciled to apartment life like her other cat, Gypsie, a Siamese. The problem was that Susan worked and couldn't be home during the day to mete out the necessary discipline to give him security.

He scratched carpets and furniture, climbed and tore drapes, promenaded on tables, counters and stove, pulled books off shelves, got into cupboards, cabinets and closets, made the opening of the apartment door into the hallway always a hazard because he was there ready to get out, and he terrorized Gypsie, who was twice his size. Apartment life was just one big frustration to Benji and he wasn't quiet about it. Recently, the neighbors had begun complaining about his raucous Burmese language. Perhaps it was just bad grammar, but the feeling seemed to be that he used Oriental obscenities unfit for most ears.

His predilection for mischief made Susan remember her sister's cat, also an apartment occupant, also an active character, who had swallowed a length of nylon thread. One end got hooked on a tooth and the normal peristaltic action of his body took the rest of it through his digestive system, twisting it about organs and guts, mangling his insides until he died in agony. The vet couldn't diagnose the problem and it took a necropsy to discover what really took place. This memory so haunted Susan that she wanted to find a place in the country where Benji could work off his surplus energy.

An article in *Psychology Today* about "Curing Peevish Pets," describes how "Man's best friend not only looks and acts like his master occasionally, but also seems to share his neuroses. A new kind of therapist treats pets with sophisticated behavioral techniques. In some cases, he must analyze the pet owner as well."

This particular therapist, a Dr. Daniel Tortora, got his Ph.D. in psychology at Michigan State University, and conducted research on animal learning and behavior there. At the time the article was written, he taught psychology at Jersey City State College and was director of an animal behavior therapy clinic in New York City's Animal Medical Center. Dr. Tortora practices as an animal behavior therapist privately in the New Jersey/New York area. He wrote the book, *Help, This Animal Is Driving Me Crazy.*

"In my practice in New Jersey and New York," he wrote, "I treat as many as 200 dogs, fifty cats, and a few other domestic animals a year." Adding, "Pets are not people, they have their own distinct psychology."

Perhaps there's the problem: every animal, human and non-human, has its own "distinct psychology." Maybe it's when people treat pets like pets that trouble begins. Often people treat their children like pets, each other like pets, like someone to fondle, pamper, order about, cage up. Is it any wonder some people go bananas?

Doctor Tortora relates several lurid cases with dogs and people. The article didn't mention any cases with cats. So, even if Susan had tried an animal psychiatrist he might not have helped her cat. Circumstances, I feel, forced her to treat Benji as a pet. She probably wasn't aware of it. Most people aren't, even when they're treating each other as pets. Susan took the only way out feasible: find a place in the country for Benji. Her parents, who live in Sonoma, thought of us.

They knew that we lived on five acres surrounded by open land. We already had three cats. Another mouth to feed couldn't be taken lightly. One of Ruth's fondest dreams was to have a Burmese cat. It was only a dream because one costs too much for free-lance writers. Now, here was a Burmese already neutered and with all his shots, being offered to us. Three cats notwithstanding, we couldn't pass up such an offer. We braced ourselves for a new cat in the family.

Susan and her folks brought Benji on a Sunday morning, set his carrier down in our family room, and opened it. He came out slowly, his light golden eyes big, reading his new surroundings. He showed not the slightest sign of freaking.

He seemed small for a two-year-old—couldn't have weighed more than six or seven pounds. I'm used to cats weighing twelve to eighteen, even twenty pounds at times. But I could see the muscles beneath his silky, cordovan-brown coat that looked black in dull daylight.

I told myself that he might be small, but there wasn't any under-nourished, uncared for look about him. It was amply obvious that Susan had done the best she could by him. It was equally obvious that he would not stand for being a pampered pet.

"He's gutsy," she said, and I could believe her.

He began to explore his new environment. Curley was the first of our cats he encountered. I expected trouble.

This oldest of our cats, with us ten years, considered himself the bouncer on the ranch. Any strange cat to appear, who wasn't a female or a kitten, found him an experienced brawler, backed by eighteen pounds that wasn't all fat.

The two approached cautiously. The Burmese gave a guttural growl, the small gleaming body lengthening, tensing, cocked for an attack or to meet an attack, all systems go. Curley replied with a mild, perhaps contemptuous hiss, and walked away with unruffled dignity, as if to say, "Oh, a kitten. Let him cool it. Maybe we'll have a game later."

Benji didn't push his questionable advantage.

His next encounter: Mao Tse-tung, asleep on the ottoman. I hoped they might be compatible because his companion in the city had been Siamese, though he hadn't gotten along with her. Now, balancing himself on his hind legs, he propped one front foot against the aqua vinyl cushion and sniffed the chocolate brown tail.

Mao seemed to come awake at once. He might have only pretended to sleep. When he saw Benji, he flared, pivoted into a defensive crouch and began making a chirping sound which I interpreted as threatening. I grabbed him. Benji settled back to the carpet and retreated beneath an end table all in slow motion.

I hadn't expected Mao's show of hostility. He's our friendliest of cats, also eighteen pounds, a plushy, good-natured softy. But there was nothing amiable about him at that moment. Perhaps, being awakened by this stranger, he felt cornered. Maybe his blue eyes met that golden Burmese stare and some race-old disagreement stirred into life.

He struggled powerfully but I held him, took him to the back door and put him outside. With a masssive show of indignation, he stalked off toward the ravine to the east. I figured he'd hunt ground squirrels or wood rats, and the foggy, damp morning would do much to cool his dudgeon.

By the time I returned to the action inside, Benji had

expanded his systematic casing of his new home, working his way from the family room to the living room three steps up. He hadn't said anything. It was hard to credit Susan's talk about his raucous voice. This place was a lot bigger than the apartment he had known in the city. Already he'd had two confrontations, two happenings. Our window walls gave him a view of a completely new and exciting world.

I watched him prowl, fascinated by the smoothness of his movements, like those of a miniaturized black leopard. Then I heard the riffle of the plastic leaves of the flexport in the utility room. Unless Mao was coming back, which I doubted, that signalled the arrival of Missy Manx. I glanced into the kitchen to make certain. Her wide, grey and white splotched face peered at me from around the refrigerator, her tassel-tipped ears listening to the strange voices of our guests. Without further concern, she went to the food dishes beneath the counter and began to eat.

As my glance returned to Benji he took a couple of scratches at the rug. Then he flowed up over the sofa to my desk, briefly examined books, papers, telephone, etc., climbed down, flowed beneath the grand piano to the wall of books, seemed to judge the vertical distance, turned quickly and flowed up to the piano bench, to the closed top of the piano. He paused again to judge the distance to the top of the bookshelves, poised to leap, hesitated.

From the kitchen came the crunching sound of dry cat food. He gave a harsh Burmese remark. The sound in the kitchen stopped.

Bookshelves forgotten, Benji came down to the rug like a wisp of spider floss and started toward the steps to the entrance hallway and the family room. Missy Manx appeared in the kitchen doorway. She saw the Burmese on the top step. For a moment her white body with its large tabby patches poised, tense. Her stumpy tail twitched angrily beneath its little ball of grey fur. Then she charged, giving the best she had in threatening hiss and spit.

Benji didn't budge. He met her expletives with a tremendous Burmese roar. Such a sound from this black character, not half her size, brought Missy to a sliding stop on the second step. She hesitated a moment, then fled. Benji held his threatening-leopard pose and didn't attack. Flight was Missy's great mistake. This third happening was over—definitely, and the Burmese had won. It was a victory Benji wasn't going to forget.

When Susan and her folks were ready to leave, I asked Sue if she had talked this move to a new home over with Benji. Without hesitation, without acting as if I were some freak to ask such a "stupid" question, both daughter and father assured me that Benji had been told over and over that he was being taken "to a new home in the country where he would have more freedom."

Their response struck me as a good sign. We can't be sure what it really means to a cat to be taken from what he has come to consider "home" and plopped down in unfamiliar and very different surroundings. We don't know what talking to a cat means to that cat—if anything but it doesn't hurt to try.

After Susan and her folks left, he seemed to like Ruth. After all, he was woman-oriented. We went to a wedding that afternoon, but a friend came in to catsit and he liked her. He growled and snarled at Mao through the window, but with people he was a very sociable, friendly feline.

By evening, he had explored the rooms. He complained a bit, looking out the windows at what, to him, was the great wonderful world outside. He used the litterbox I had fixed for him and even made a tentative show of eating. It was only a show because he wasn't ready to settle in yet.

We closed the flexport so he couldn't get out. Ruth joked, "He might decide to go back to San Francisco."

A cat returning to his former home is not unusual but we felt from what Susan had said that his dislike of his former home would rule out any such attempt.

In our family room the TV stands on a dolly beside the fireplace and the stereo cabinet is against the opposite wall. At dinner time I turned on the stereo. Benji looked at the TV, went to it and leaped smoothly to the top. Apparently he was accustomed to sleeping atop Susan's TV and he associated music and voices with it. When the TV didn't warm up and sound came from across the room, he seemed puzzled. Later when I turned on the tube and the screen lit and sound came, he seemed to relax a little—that was the way things should be. The closeness of the TV to the fireplace bothered him. He didn't know about crackling flames. He watched, then got down, prowled a little, groused a little, then settled himself on the plum-colored blanket I had folded for him on the couch.

Curley and Mao came in, ate and napped. The red tabby hardly seemed to notice Benji. The Siamese and the Burmese seemed at a stand-off. We let Mao and Missy Manx sleep in our bedroom that first night. Curley curled up as usual on his chair by the fireplace. Benji was still on the couch when we went to bed.

The situation looked promising. But we left Benji's carrier with its red cushion on a chair behind a folding partition. Its door was open. In the morning Ruth found him asleep on it. Undoubtedly it meant a contact with Sue and security to him.

Our three regular cats were fed in the kitchen as usual at breakfast time. Benji made no move to join them. He still wasn't ready to eat. After finishing their breakfast, the regulars went out, did what they had to do and asked to come in again because the flexport was closed. All three settled down for their customary morning naps. Even Missy Manx found a place up by my desk to sleep.

Benji did little napping. He left his sanctuary in the carrier later in the morning, explored a bit, checked the location of the other cats, used his litterbox, climbed on the washer and the window ledge above it to look into the carport and complained a bit. Ever alert and ready for an encounter, Benji gradually relaxed when the other cats didn't threaten him. He still didn't eat more than a nibble of dry food and drank only a little milk.

That afternoon Ruth took him out for the first time. He had never been beyond an apartment hallway before and the world of the country was full of happenings. There was grass to experience, fallen leaves that rustled and shifted in the wind, and objects swooping overhead, making him drop to the ground in a reflex couch. His eyes explored everything, his twitching nose working overtime but he always stayed close to Ruth.

When she sat on the deck in the sun he amused himself catching flies since flies were all he had to catch in the apartment. He soon learned that a bee was not a fly and that the autumn chill was different from the even temperature of a San Francisco flat. Apparently the sunlight seldom shone into Susan's apartment so he didn't know about the warmth from that bright thing up there in the blue. Sunlight and shade seemed to puzzle him. He moved in and out of them on the deck, and finally he wandered off to do some exploring on his own. That was the first time he was completely free in the wide world of the country.

Ruth called him when she was ready to go and he came at once. "I guess he hasn't decided yet to go back to the city," she said, and we laughed. That small Burmese feline had more excitement and exercise that afternoon than ever before.

When it grew dark, he wanted out again. After all, the night was made for cats—especially black cats like Benji. He grumbled a little when we wouldn't let him out. The kids came trick-or-treating and Ruth carried him to the door and let them pet him. That to him was another happening. He was a perfect Halloween cat, calm and fearless in the presence of weird-costumed youngsters.

After the kids went their way, Ruth brought him into the family room and put him on the stereo. The cabinet top was warm and music flowed from the speaker. He sniffed the top, pondered, then showed signs of understanding the relationship between warmth, sound and source. Later when I pulled the TV into the room and turned it on and the stereo off, he changed his sleep spot to the familiar one above the picture screen.

That second night he again slept in his carrier. He seemed more at home the next day, even climbed on the counters several times and was scolded. The third night he slept on the plum-colored blanket on the couch and the other cats slept in their customary places.

Now Benji's relationship with the three established felines began to change and develop. Perhaps because he was smaller he suffered from the "little guy" syndrome. On every opportunity he challenged Mao and Curley.

Curley refused to take offense. Several times I watched the Burmese stalk him, growling threateningly, daring him to fight. The red tabby just looked puzzled, as if thinking, "This kid's gotta be nuts. What's he trying to quarrel with me for?" Once I actually saw Curley look over his shoulder as if he thought the Burmese was threatening some cat behind him.

With Mao it was different; Ruth's lap was his. Being woman-oriented, Benji wanted it too. If she weren't in her recliner and her lap wasn't available they wanted to sleep on the red cushions. That situation produced some near battles. Besides, Mao was always looking for someone to play a game with. He responded to Benji's threats with a chirping sound as if to say, "You wanna play, let's play." But the Burmese always made a slow, dignified retreat.

They rarely came to blows. Once I saw them testing each other on the carhood. It didn't seem serious. Later I heard a brawl on the outside of the wall of ivy that forms one side of the carport. When I arrived to stop the fight, Benji was picking himself up from among fallen leaves. Mao stood over him bristling indignantly. A patch of the ivy dripped and Mao's side showed wet. Trying to reconstruct the encounter I concluded that Mao had been doing a spray job when the Burmese breached cat protocol and jumped him. Perhaps Mao had a right to be furious. Neither appeared to be any the worse for the encounter.

It didn't take Benji long to learn that he couldn't push Mao around the way he had Gypsie in San Francisco. Outdoors they sometimes played, chasing each other, but not really getting serious. Ruth concluded that Benji felt that he could out-run Mao in the open.

During rainy weather the cats didn't get much exercise and

Mao would try to promote a game with Benji in the house. He would lie on his side and roll and wriggle toward the Burmese, making little mewing sounds as if to say, "Aw, come on, let's wrestle." Benji only growled and backed off. Sometimes a brawl would start and one or the other of us would have to yell, "Hey, you guys, knock it off!"

Indoors when it rained all of Benji's bad habits came out. He walked on tables and counters. Once he stole a piece of pot roast. He took his prize to the spot beneath the counter where cats were fed. Another time Ruth gave him some ends of cooked chicken wings. She put them on the paper by the cats' dishes. He took them to the bowl of dry cat food and ate them in it. Another time he stole a small bone from a pork roast. I first saw it on the floor. Later it too had been put in the dry cat food bowl.

He seemed to hunt mischief. Open a door, any door, and he would dash through, no matter where it led. If a cupboard door was open a crack, he would pry it wide enough for him to get inside. He climbed into the washer and dryer if their doors were open. We always had to be careful when we used either to make sure he wasn't inside. He jumped from shelf to shelf in the utility room until he reached the top.

Any attempt to discipline him was a joke. When he was on a counter, or into some place where he shouldn't be, a yell, "Benji!" scared him off or out—eventually. If one or the other of us were close enough to whack him, he wouldn't say anything, but he'd wash the spot smacked, then come and roll against our ankles. He didn't get mad at us. It was all a game.

If he climbed onto a counter without our noticing he'd bray, "Arrrrrragh!" to attract our attention. He wasn't defiant, just having fun.

When the weather cleared and cats could go out to play and hunt, he didn't get into as much mischief indoors. Now when we said, "Maybe he's decided to go back to San Francisco," we were really joking. We had no fear that something like that might happen.

Meanwhile, the friction between Benji and Missy Manx increased. The fact that he had won at their first meeting may have told him he could bully her. Maybe he didn't view her as a cat. He had probably never seen a Manx in his life. Her stumpy tail put her in a different class.

When she first came to us, that characteristic had puzzled both Curley and Mao. They sniffed it whenever they had a chance. When our grandson first saw her, he made a point of checking out both Curley and Mao to see if they had standard tails. We don't know how Missy felt about it. I always joked that she had "tail envy." As for Benji, maybe this nonconformity gave her no right in the house or around the ranch.

Outside, he paced around in front of her in a threatening manner but as long as she didn't run he didn't attack. Sometimes they'd just sit a few feet apart staring at each other until one arose slowly and walked off carefully.

Missy still came into the house but she avoided Benji. In good weather she spent the nights out, then came in at breakfast, ate and napped. One day she decided to sleep on the blanket on the couch that Benji had appropriated as his bed. He paced around glaring but didn't try to dislodge her. But he no longer slept on that blanket. That stumped-tailed creature had defiled his sacred Burmese bed.

He took to threatening her openly. In a very short time she was afraid to come in to eat or sleep. We let her into our bedroom through the patio door from the bath. She slept on our beds and we fed her in the bathroom.

However, if we were out for the evening, she sometimes slipped into the kitchen for a snack. Once Benji caught her there. When we got home we found broken dishes and spilled food, and gobs of grey and white fur scattered about the kitchen floor. Missy didn't suffer much damage. With her thick double coat she could afford to lose a little fur.

Benji had proven to himself, at least, that this strange-looking, tailless, grey and white character, wasn't to be allowed into his house if he could help it.

At Christmas time our seven-year-old grandson, Alex, visited us. Benji had never been around a youngster before. At first he was a little shy, but soon Alex was carrying him around, dragging a toy on a string for him to chase. After

Alex went home, Benji was content to just curl up and rest for several days; no counter hopping, no cupboard invading, no mischief at all.

Susan and her folks dropped in to see Benji. We told Sue that all she had needed to make the Burmese into a docile apartment cat was a seven-year-old youngster. Benji was glad to see Susan. He hadn't forgotten her, and didn't seem to resent her giving him away. When she sat on the floor, he rubbed against her, and took a curling, head-down spill into her lap. She brought him three plastic balls with tiny bells in each. He batted these about the family room with a violent exuberance that could be easily interpreted as pleasure at seeing her.

She didn't visit often and the following summer he showed that he missed her. Another young friend of ours, a little older than Susan but just about her build, stopped in one day. The plastic toys Susan had given Benji had been put on a tray beside the TV long ago. He could play with them any time. Whenever he got on or off the TV he went past them but hadn't played with them for months.

After dinner Winnie, our friend, and Ruth and I were talking in the family room and Benji joined us. Winnie talked to him, petted him and he performed his curling dive against her ankle. She invited him into her lap but he didn't stay. Instead, he hopped up on the TV dolly, hooked one of the plastic toys out of the tray and began batting it about the room with incredible fury. He kept this up for ten minutes or more. When tired, he curled into Winnie's lap and fell into an exhausted sleep as if she were perhaps a surrogate Susan. Something triggered his memory of a very nice young woman who had been his owner and companion and some exciting evenings they spent together.

My imagination? Maybe. His actions were quite different from any behavior shown before when we had company.

Shortly after he arrived we made sure he knew how to use the flexport. If he ran into trouble outside, he could always get into the house and safety. That winter as his world of happenings expanded he never seemed to get into that kind of trouble. Benji dished out trouble.

Our young tenant had a red tabby almost the color of Curley. His name was Burgie. He was twice the size of the Burmese but shy. He fled at the sight of Benji, and in spite of his resemblance to Curley, Benji chased him. Burgie became adept at avoiding all of our cats. But it was part of Benji's world of happenings to patrol the apartment area, crossing the terrace in front regularly, hoping to see the red tabby through the window. Once he came upon Burgie in the woods below the apartment and immediately gave chase.

They tangled and snarled and rolled over and over on the ground. Burgie took to the nearest tree but Benji wasn't used to climbing up trees, at least not in a pursuit situation. He hesitated, finally concluded that he could do anything Burgie could do and went up after him. They clenched on a limb and fell off, landing on the ground "plop."

Burgie had more experience with trees and landed running. It was a first for Benji so he received a considerable jolt, came in through the flexport and was somewhat subdued for an hour or so.

A bigger happening for him was his encounter with a horse. Another time when Ruth took him for a walk down the drive, the horse we were keeping was at the gate near the pumphouse. As usual Benji showed no fear. He ducked under the fence and sniffed the horse's hooves. This didn't bother the horse, she was used to cats, but she put her nose down to read this small black character taking liberties with her feet. Then she blew out her breath with a whooffling sound from her nostrils. A black streak was Benji, going beneath the fence and back to the flexport and into the house.

After each such new happening, we laughed and speculated, "He probably just shakes his head and thinks, 'Susan never told me the country was going to be like this'." In no time after washing himself and eating, he'd head back out the flexport looking for newer and bigger happenings.

The greatest of all happenings came the night Mao caught a

rabbit that had been ravaging our spring garden. Benji had seen other cats—even strange ones like Missy Manx, if he considered her feline. He had demolished them all, or at least tried to. He knew about dogs—"Hold me back, I'll kill 'em." He knew that a horse-monster could blow him away in a breath. A rabbit he'd never seen. We doubted that he'd seen a squirrel, rat or even a mouse. We were sure he'd never seen a rabbit. He was an underprivileged city apartment cat.

It was late February and rain had been coming down in torrents. I was watching TV. Ruth had fallen asleep in her recliner with Benji stretched out on her lap. Curley was in his chair by the fireplace. I knew that Missy Manx was dry in our bedroom.

Sometime after ten o'clock I heard a cat come in and automatically assured myself that it was Mao. The first inkling I had that something wasn't normal about his homecoming was when he came to my chair and "merrped." I reached down to pet him and realized that he was soaked—absolutely soaked.

My interest in the tube ceased. Here was Mao, who hated rain like no other cat in the world, so soaked that he might have been dunked in a barrel of water. He didn't seem aware of it; he certainly didn't seem to care. My first thought was to get a towel and try to dry him off.

The moment I moved he let out a louder "merrp" and raced to the hallway between the bedrooms and baths, I followed and turned on the light. There lay a dead rabbit—a brush bunny or a young jackrabbit. How he'd managed to carry it in there without my being aware of it was a mystery. The TV program couldn't have been *that* good. Of course, the rabbit was as soaked as Mao. Its ears were plastered down, and the white undercoat of hair showed through the bedraggled outer grey fur.

Mao didn't even know he was soaked. The most important thing to him at that moment was his catch, his great triumph. He was wildly ecstatic. This was his first catch in weeks. He came and rubbed against me. He went over and sniffed the rabbit. He chirruped and miaowed and chittered. I told him how wonderful he was, what a mighty hunter—probably the greatest in the world. I poured on praise as thick as cream.

Then I realized that Benji crouched just inside the hallway staring at the rabbit. Mao went to him and rubbed his wet side across Benji's face. Benji, who didn't like wet any more than Mao never flinched or made a sound. The Siamese returned to the rabbit, shook it, and laid it down. He seemed to be offering his prize to Benji. The Burmese, at that moment, had become an obsidian statue with bulging, staring pale golden eyes.

I picked up the rabbit by a hind foot and took it to the family room beneath the corner table where our cats have eaten their catches during inclement weather for fifteen years. Mao followed, and as soon as I put the rabbit down, he began tossing it around in a fresh display of triumph.

The commotion had aroused Ruth and she played her role, pouring on fulsome praise. I don't know, perhaps Mao had had enough glory, or maybe his hunger had caught up with him. He began tearing at the grey-white body, preparing to dine. Then I noticed Benji's enormous, staring eyes hiding beneath my chair.

Mao crunched away until he had his fill, then came out into the room and began washing and drying himself. By this time Curley had come to see what was going on. He took in the situation and went to the remains of the rabbit. With a shake of it, a gesture of establishing his right, he began to chomp away.

In our cat hierarchy, Curley was Benji's best friend. Unlike Mao and the Burmese, the red tabby and Benji had no points of conflict. So Curley moved in on what was left of the rabbit, and the Burmese came out of his safe-place, following, stopping just short of a yard from the action.

He stared at Curley a moment, then backed off slowly and fled across the room beneath the couch. He stopped to stare, but only an instant before flowing out and up to the top of the couch back. After a moment's hesitation, he retreated to the far end where he resumed the pose of a shiny, obsidian statue, watching Curley crunching at the carcass of the rabbit beneath the table.

Rabbit? It was then I began wondering what Benji made of all this. In his frame of reference I realized that there was probably not a single rabbit. In his frame of reference there was only one grey and white animal without a tail. Missy Manx!

Had Mao caught Missy Manx? From a catseye level that bedraggled grey and white creature he watched Mao and Curley consume, might have looked like the grey and white interloper he had chased and fought with. Maybe she wasn't another cat. Or maybe those two monster cats didn't make any distinction. Cat or not?

"Great Cat Goddess, Bastet! Susan never told me country living was like this! Cannibalism? Nothing short of cannibalism!"

At that moment Curley decided to finish off what little was left of Mao's catch in front of the fireplace. I felt that permissiveness had gone far enough and took the pieces of grey and white fur and a couple of feet out to the carport. Curley followed dutifully.

When I returned, Benji crouched still a stone statue at the end of the couch. Now he stared at Mao who had moved over to the rug to dry himself.

Perhaps, at that moment, for the first time, Mao's size meant something to the seven-pound Benji. "Will I be next? Will those monstrous country cats catch me and eat me? Have they just been waiting their chance?"

There's no way of knowing what went on in the small Burmese brain. And more's the pity. But we had a good laugh. We felt sure this happening had shaken every fiber of Benji's small body. Maybe we over-reacted anthropomorphically, but in the morning, our speculations were revived when we noticed the Burmese make a wide detour around Mao and Curley on his way to the kitchen. He ate alone. By midday he seemed to have accepted this latest happening. His boldness returned. Maybe he felt convinced that he was big enough to handle those two giant country cats. After all, he'd routed Missy Manx himself, the first day here, and he'd driven her out of the house later. "Why, I might have caught her myself,

with a little luck." And he'd beaten up that red tabby downstairs.

The weather cleared and that afternoon Ruth took Benji,
Mao and Curley for their usual walk down the drive. They
played, pouncing each other, chasing and being chased, climbing trees. And Benji's apprehensions, if any, seemed put
away.

About four-thirty, knowing that Benji was out, I let Missy
Manx leave the bedroom. She went to the place beneath the
kitchen counter where cats ate and I fed her. When she
finished, she went to the back door and wanted out.

The flexport is beside that door but our cats won't use it if
a human is available to open the people's door. Above the
flexport on the outside I had built a shelf to make the entrance a little less conspicuous to strange animals.

I opened the back door and Missy marched out. From the
corner of my eye I saw Benji crouching on that shelf. For a
moment, I held my breath, thinking I had let the Manx into a
trap. I expected the Burmese to jump her at once. But Missy
set out purposefully across the carport to the steps to the
woodlot and the field beyond. Benji didn't move. He was a
stone statue again, nose and ears and big eyes pointing after
the gray and white character crossing the cement, her stumpy
tail twitching saucily. It wasn't until she had passed a rick of
cordwood that he cautiously climbed off his shelf and followed. He made no attempt to give chase. He kept a safe
distance behind, using steps, and chunks of wood, and the
bole of a live oak tree to cover his pursuit. He didn't travel
beyond the end of the cordwood.

To have known what went on in his mind at that moment
could change the world. I went up to the deck where Ruth sat
in the sun. "Benji," I said, "has just seen the ghost of Missy
Manx." I told her what had happened and we laughed loudly
about it.

The thought is still good for a chuckle.

Benji recovered from this happening too. He even returned
to feuding with Missy, and on occasion, threatening Mao—
and sometimes his good friend Curley. Perhaps he has con-

cluded, "The country's a rougher place than I dreamed. The happenings are wild here. But happenings is what life is all about—especially for a Burmese cat. And this is my home. I'm stayin'."

If he ever remembers the security and comfort of Susan's apartment, and I'm sure he does when the right circumstances program the retrieval from his memory bank, I don't think he ever wishes he were back in San Francisco. At times, I wonder if he wishes beyond bigger and wilder happenings.

Benji is all cat. He may be a people too. But he's not a pet to me. He's my friend just as the other cats are my friends. I worry about him more, perhaps, mostly because he never had the advantage of living in the country during that crucial two-to-five months of kittenhood. I fear that he may meet problems he cannot handle—a rattlesnake maybe. I fear that his search for happenings may lead him farther and farther afield into dangers and misadventures.

Once he disappeared for three days. We thought he must be lost but found him on the roof of a new house under construction within a couple of hundred yards of our back door. How he got there or why, we don't know. When I searched the neighborhood and that place the first day he was gone, why didn't I find him?

Mao perhaps knows. When I brought Benji home that evening and he and the Siamese met in our kitchen, both lay down and rolled. They opened their mouths wide as if in great silent laughter. Maybe it was relaxation and relief at meeting again. And maybe it was some colossal joke that only they knew about.

He may disappear again. Shutting him in the house or keeping him in an apartment is not the answer. If I had the knowledge and the intelligence to communicate with him— with all of my cats—what an exciting world to be a part of. All I can do is my best to see that he and the others are protected, pray to the Great Cat Goddess for help, and keep my fingers crossed.